PURCHASING AND COSTING FOR THE HOSPITALITY INDUSTRY

DENISE DRUMMOND

Hodder & Stoughton

A MEMBER OF THE HODDER HEADLINE GROUP

Order queries: please contact Bookpoint Ltd, 39 Milton Park, Abingdon, Oxon OX14 4TD.
Telephone: (44) 01235 400414, Fax: (44) 01235 400454. Lines are open from 9.00–6.00, Monday to
Saturday, with a 24 hour message answering service. Email address: orders@bookpoint.co.uk.

British Library Cataloguing in Publication Data
A catalogue record for this title is available from The British Library

ISBN 0 340 68833 5 ✓

First published 1998
Impression number   10   9   8   7   6   5   4   3   2   1
Year   2003   2002   2001   2000   1999   1998

Copyright © 1998 Denise Drummond

Typeset by Wearset, Boldon, Tyne and Wear.
Printed in Great Britain for Hodder & Stoughton Educational, a division of Hodder Headline Plc,
338 Euston Road, London NW1 3BH by Redwood Books, Trowbridge, Wiltshire.

Contents

Introduction

This book is intended for students studying on GNVQ, BTEC Diploma and HND courses and for owners/operators in the hospitality business. It is a basic introduction designed for those who are new to or who don't understand purchasing and costing.

Whichever aspect of the hospitality business you intend to pursue, you cannot expect to create an impact unless you understand the financial mechanics of costing, pricing, purchasing and control.

How good an operator or a manager you are, or your success as a team member in the hospitality business, will be determined by many factors, but undoubtedly one of the main criteria for judging your success will be your ability as an individual or a team member to deliver a satisfactory profit at the end of the day.

Businesses nowadays will only survive if they make money. If you don't make money, you can't pay your bills. It is no longer good enough in this business to create fabulous dishes in the kitchen and to have a wonderful personality 'out front' or to be blessed with 'being good with people' unless the department or establishment in which you work makes an acceptable profit.

If you work for any organisation that does not have effective costing and purchasing policies, you will not have a job for long, and that business will survive on a 'wing and a prayer' and from 'day to day'. Being part of something successful is infinitely more fun. Of course, you've got to keep the customers satisfied and keep them coming through the door – but this must be done **profitably**.

The financing and controlling of your department or establishment isn't difficult to understand. Time spent now learning about costing and pricing and how to monitor performance from week to week, month to month or year to year will make your job easier and your department or establishment more profitable.

1
Making Your Purchasing Professional: The Purchasing Cycle

Importance of planning

Any successful business must plan to be financially successful. Part of this planning process lies in the purchasing plan of the business. It is not just a question of picking up the telephone and ordering. In the hospitality business purchasing should involve continually monitoring to ensure that both you and the customer are achieving value for money. Your main aim should be to provide goods and services within a given budget (that is, the price charged). In order to do this, you should:

- be selecting suppliers who give value for money;
- let the suppliers know what standard you expect of them;
- plan a simple system for ordering, checking and receiving goods;
- plan a reliable system where you can store products safely and control their exit to the various points of sale in your establishment.

Good purchasing will get the right products in the right place at the right time. Remember that you are the customer in this situation and that you can, within reason, dictate your requirements to your suppliers. The chances are they want your business in the same way that you want your customers' business. So, the planning process should involve the following:

■ selecting a supplier;
■ ordering;
■ delivery and storage;
■ monitoring.

Before selecting a supplier, you need to establish a list of what you will require. You will require items for your menu, wines for your wine list, cleaning agents for housekeeping, conference supplies, office supplies and so on. Make sure that all of this will fit the identified needs of your customers and decide on the quality of goods you wish to order.

Quality

By identifying the needs of your customers, you will have compiled a menu suitable for the market in which you will be operating.

Let's decide on the quality of mushrooms to be used in a Garlic Mushroom starter. What does the recipe call for? There are many different types of mushrooms on the market which vary in size, shape, colour and price. If we decide that there will be 2oz of mushrooms per portion of garlic mushrooms, then we should be selecting small mushrooms (psychologically 8 or 9 small mushrooms presented as a portion will be better received by the customer than 2 or 3 large mushrooms).

So, button mushrooms (rather than flat cap, oyster, shitake or chanterelle) would be most suitable. Perhaps we should specify small, button mushrooms which should be firm and fresh and retain their shape during preparation and cooking. You may be able to accept larger mushrooms, perhaps a day or two older, if you are using them to make mushroom soup which will be liquidised and where quality is less important.

Selecting beef burgers can be a daunting task when you realise the number of beef burgers which are on the market. One of the best ways of doing this is to obtain 5 or 6 samples, cook them off and taste them blind with a panel of 3 or 4 people. I did this recently with a client who was introducing beef burger and chips to his menu and the panel's decision was unanimous – the winner was the most expensive of the burgers the panel tasted, but we all agreed it 'smacked of quality' and tasted delicious.

Quantity

Once the quality has been decided, look at the quantity you are going to order at any one time or, indeed, over a given period. This will involve you making decisions on what stock levels you wish to hold which, in turn, will be determined by the forecasts of business levels. In addition, you need to look at the frequency and timing of deliveries. You don't need to buy a massive quantity (for example, three weeks' supply of goods) if your supplier can deliver them freshly to you two, three or four times a week. If you do buy more than you have to, you are over-stocked and you are piling money onto the shelves, which might otherwise be in the bank. In addition, you have to ask yourself whether or not goods kept in your storage conditions for longer than is necessary will be in prime condition when your customer receives them.

You will also need to consider the storage spaces available in cellars, fridges, chills, freezers or stock rooms. How much you order, the quality of what you order, and the frequency in which you order will have a direct effect on your budget and cash flows. It is very often the case that the price you pay will be reflected in the quantity of purchasing in that there are normally discounts for quantity.

Likewise, minor quality adjustments may achieve savings also. It goes without saying that where goods are subject to market fluctuations, for example fresh foodstuffs, your prices will fluctuate accordingly. You therefore expect your suppliers to pass on the low prices in the same way they pass on the high prices.

The hospitality business involves three main sales activities:
- food sales;
- drinks sales;
- accommodation sales.

Where food and beverage is concerned, the goods have to be purchased, held in stock and then sold. Once this cycle has been completed, the process starts all over again and is repeated as often as possible. In fact, the more times it happens, and the cycle is completed, the busier your establishment is, and therefore the more profit you should be attracting and accumulating in your bank. It's a buy/store/sell cycle.

Let's follow the buy/store/sell cycle of a gin and tonic. It is relatively easy to source a supplier of spirits and a supplier of soft drinks and many suppliers will offer a total drinks service, that is, wines, spirits, beers and soft drinks.

Gin can be purchased in many sizes of bottles, and where turnover is high, many cases will be bought in the one order. The cardboard 'outers' or cases of gin will be placed in the appropriate cellar 'bin' where they will remain until they are requisitioned by any of the bars requiring supply. Once requisitioned, the gin is either securely stored in or near the bar, or on the bar gantry, from where it is dispensed or sold. Then the cycle starts all over again. How much gin and tonic you sell will depend on how often the above cycle is completed.

Like any other commercial activity, you sell the food and drink for a greater price than you paid for the raw materials, and the difference between the buying price and the selling price is called the **gross profit**.

Where accommodation is concerned, the cycle is a little different. You don't go around buying and selling rooms, you only sell them. Travel Agents and room booking agencies are the people who buy and sell rooms. How does the room cycle work and what makes it fundamentally different from the food and beverage operations?

Where accommodation is concerned, it's a sell/sell/sell cycle. Why? Because if you don't sell a gin and tonic today, you will still have it in stock to sell tomorrow. If you don't sell a portion of lamb cutlets today, they will stay in the chill until tomorrow and you can sell them then. But if you don't sell a room tonight, you have lost that revenue for ever.

If you have a 20 bedroom hotel, then every night you have 20 rooms to sell.

Let's look at the night of Friday 13 June 1997, and let's assume that at the weekend rooms are £50 each.

Potentially, you have revenue of $20 \times 50 = £1000$, but you only sell 6 rooms, so the revenue is only £300. The remaining revenue of £700 is lost for ever because there will never be another 13 June 1997!

So in this 20 bedroom hotel, the total bedroom availability throughout the year is $20 \times 365 = 7300$ rooms. The cycle will be completed if, in a year, you can sell 7300 rooms. In theory, this is possible, but in practice it seldom, if ever happens.

So we have to adopt a different method of costing and selling our rooms than we do for costing and selling our food and beverage. More of this in Chapter 10.

Being successful in these buying and selling transactions and creating enough profit for the business will be determined by many aspects of your business, most notably:
■ the buying price of the items;
■ the number of items you sell;
■ the selling price of the items you sell;
■ the mix of items you sell.

This will determine the amount of money that flows into your bank account (sales) and out of your bank account (purchases and expenses).

Any operation in the hospitality industry will need to buy goods or services which will generally fall into three distinct categories:
1 Goods for direct re-sale such as food and beverages.
2 Goods and services without which an operator could not operate such as gas, electricity, wages, cleaning materials, waiter's cloths, more teaspoons (when you're down to your last 10!).
3 Beds, carpets, kitchen equipment, vans, cars, computers, once again without which an operator could not operate.

The point here is that food and beverage are bought in **1** for the sole purpose of being re-sold to your customers at a profit which is great enough to pay for **2** so that after profits have been made you will have retained enough money to replace the type of goods in **3**. After all, beds, carpets, kitchen equipment, motor vehicles and computers have a limited life in that they do not go on for ever – they need replacing and that costs money.

The purchasing cycle

So let's look at how, when and where you buy your goods. The purchasing cycle is pivotal to overall business performance and a firm purchasing policy is the initial control point of the business. Figure 1.1 shows the purchasing cycle.

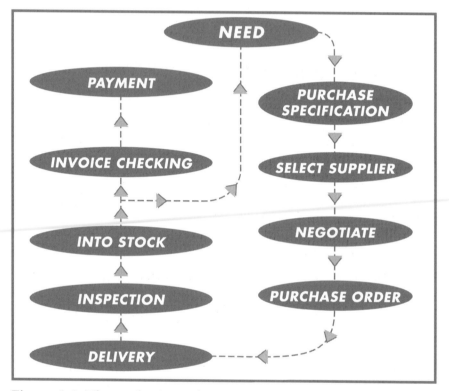

Figure 1.1 *The purchasing cycle*

The purchasing cycle (See Figure 1.1)

- **Need** (recipe/wine list) – what market are we in; fast food, staff catering, à la carte restaurant, café, bistro, and so on
- **Purchase Specification**
- **Select supplier** (short list)
- **Negotiate** – price, quantities, delivery frequency
- **Purchase Order** – raise the initial paperwork which will allow your supplier to initialise your order
- **Delivery**
- **Inspection**

■ **Into stock** – for as short a time as possible
■ **Invoice checking**
■ **Payment to supplier**

Let's examine each element of the purchasing cycle in more detail.

Need

Purchasing considerations

■ What market are we in?
■ What quantity (bulk) will we be buying?
■ How much will customers pay for a specific dish or menu?
■ How much are we prepared to pay for the raw materials?
■ What size of portion will they expect?
■ What additional items will be on the plate, for instance garnish?
■ What style of service? Plated? Silver?
■ How much profit do we need to make?
■ Will we buy fresh or frozen poultry?
■ What are the factors to be considered when buying fresh or frozen?
■ How many of these specific dishes will we sell in a meal service, in a day, in a week, in a month?

These are just some of the questions we will have to ask. All these questions need clear, concise answers, so we must make clear policies which will determine much of the decision making in the purchasing questions we have posed.

These policies will be further determined by the scale of the organisation.

Know your market and therefore know your customer needs. Keep the needs of your customer at the front of your mind all the time. If a dish on the menu is *not* selling, find out why. It might be something to do with your purchasing policy.

Purchase Specification

A Purchase Specification is a written description of any item which you purchase on a regular basis. It will eliminate the possibility of incorrect goods being delivered, or goods of an inferior standard. It avoids misunderstandings and helps ensure consistency of standards of delivered items. A date will communicate to your supplier that it is the most up-to-date specification for the item, and it is the one he should be supplying to.

Like any paperwork in the purchasing cycle, a date should always be present, as Purchase Specifications will change.

Figure 1.2 shows an example of a purchase specification.

Central Square Hotels Limited
26 The Strand, Manchester MC9 4BU
Tel: 0161 204 5959 Ext. 32

Purchase Specification:	PO2 01/04/199..
Commodity:	Frozen Chicken Supreme
Size:	7 ozs
Quality:	Plump
Origin:	British
Weight:	14lbs, approx. 32 per case
Quote:	per Case
Delivery:	Tuesday or Friday following order
Notice to Supplier:	Frozen foods will only be accepted on delivery if the temperature is between -12 degrees C and -15 degrees C

Figure 1.2 *Purchase Specification*

Select supplier

In the larger organisations Purchase Specifications will be sent out to a number of selected suppliers, in order for the company to obtain competitive quotations from each supplier.

In reality though, you would aim to buy from a few rather than many suppliers as it is easier to administer and therefore more cost effective.

Buyers should thoroughly investigate all potential suppliers before contacting them for quotations.

Nowadays, many suppliers of goods and services have a commitment to quality, manifested by an appropriate quality endorsement, for example ISO 2000. This will often sway a buyer because he or she will know that a commitment of quality from a supplier will guarantee a high standard of goods and services.

Hospitality businesses will buy from a range of sources:
- Manufacturer/Producer;
- Trade Markets, for example Meat Market, Fish Market, Vegetable Market;
- Wholesalers;
- One-Stop-Shop Catering Suppliers;
- Cash and Carry.

Where a business buys their goods will depend upon some or all of the following:
- **Geographical location** – you will have a far greater choice of suppliers if you operate from a large town or city or are near centres of population linked by a motorway or trunk road.
- **Proximity to any of the above** – the further you are from the main markets or distribution points, the further you will have to travel to buy and the less frequent your deliveries will be. It will be less likely that you will have, for example, a next-day delivery, so you will have to carry your stock for longer.
- **Buying policy** – there is no credit facility with a Cash and Carry, which means you have to pay for the goods before you sell them. This will affect your cash flow, in as much as the money you pay out for your supplies will be out of your bank before your customers pay you for the goods and services you are selling.
- **Size of business** – remember, there is almost always more than one option, and nowadays there can be a marketing edge gained by businesses who use and promote fresh goods from local suppliers.

Initiatives such as Taste of England, Ireland, Scotland and Wales, and more recently in Scotland, The Natural Cooking of Scotland, will help business source suppliers.

■ **Price** – this is probably the biggest consideration for any business deciding where to source goods, but beware of buying the cheapest on the market. If quality is to be compromised, your customers will notice.

How many of us have eaten breakfast made up of the cheapest sausages and bacon on the market?

Beware also of buying in bulk in order to achieve discount. You must have the business demand, the cash flow and adequate storage facilities.

Do your customers really want to eat pork chops that have been in the freezer for 3 months? What about your overdraft?

Negotiate

Get to know your suppliers and explain your buying policy/philosophy to them. Your suppliers are in the business of **SELLING** and they will sell for as great a profit as they can make. They will discount, but only if they're asked. There is a price below which they cannot go otherwise they will sell at a loss, which isn't really the reason for being in business.

In fact, their attitude to you should be very similar to your attitude to your customers – you want their business, but not at *any* price.

At the point of negotiation, let your suppliers know when they will get paid by you. If you look after your suppliers, they will look after you, and remember, if you are a smaller business, that spending 20 minutes every day haggling over the price of a box of tomatoes is perhaps time you could be spending doing something else. Make it your business to read the market pages of trade magazines, such as *Caterer and Hotelkeeper* and use 'this time last year' as an indicator to seasonal price fluctuations for example. Remember that the old practice of changing the menu 4 times per year was to reflect the seasonal goods of winter, spring, summer and autumn. This also reflects the seasonal prices of these foods.

I recently worked with a large Direct Services Organisation who were told by their fruit and vegetable supplier that neither Ogen melons nor broccoli were in season in May! Whether a particular fruit or vegetable is in season nowadays is hardly relevant. In the 1990s almost anything can be found by a keen and reputable supplier if the notice period and price are right!

Purchase Order

This is the 'end of the beginning of the purchasing cycle'. At this point, you, the purchaser, are entering into an agreement with your supplier to purchase certain goods. The purchase order is also the point at which goods start to move and therefore financial responsibilities start to change.

Once a supplier receives a Purchase Order, the wheels crank into motion.

A Purchase Order is an official order and is usually on a pre-printed form.

The large multi-national companies will have pre-printed forms, usually triplicate or quadruplicate colour coded and sequentially numbered Purchase Order forms.

The independent operator may well use a pre-numbered duplicate book – the ones where you tear off the top copy and send it to the supplier and keep the copy in the book. If you use this system, it is a good idea to have a stamp made so that your name, address and telephone number is on the top of the page. It looks much more professional.

Alternatively, the smaller businesses who use PCs will find that designing a Purchase Order (P/O) form is simple and they can be generated from the computer or bulk photocopied from one original the next time you are passing a high street copy shop. Remember that if you are generating your own P/O stationery then you will have to number each P/O according to your own system. The idea of having sequential order numbers is to ensure that only official orders are made to suppliers. Otherwise, think what might happen if the purchasing was not controlled. Things could be ordered from anybody, right, left and centre!

11

When the goods which have been ordered by using an official P/O arrive at their designated destination, the official P/O number will appear on the delivery note/advice note, which always accompanies the goods being delivered, and thus the first part of the financial control cycle is in place.

If the P/O number referred to on the delivery or advice note is not one which has originated from the official ordering department, further investigation (such as signature of authorised purchaser) will reveal that the order is unofficial.

Figure 1.3 shows an example of a Purchase Order.

An official Purchase Order will contain the following information:

1 the name and address of the purchasers (normally pre-printed, or stamped with an 'official' stamp);
2 the name and address of the supplier to whom the P/O is being sent;
3 an order number – this might be sequential (45, 46, 47, and so on) as each order is sent out, or it might also contain departmental codes, with each department raising its own Purchase Order, for example:
Banqueting – BQ0104, BQ0105
Housekeeping – HK2854, HK2855
Kitchen – KT749, KT750
4 the date the Purchase Order was raised;
5 a brief description of the goods required giving quantities, where appropriate;
6 any other relevant information such as delivery instructions, delivery dates and times, and so on;
7 price – as per supplier;
8 total price of order.

Where 7 and 8 are concerned, there is a school of thought which states that prices should **not** appear on official orders, but if you have already negotiated/discussed the price with your supplier, it is an extra 'control' which will avoid any misunderstanding and save time all round.

9 Authorised signatory with name pre-printed or name hand-written in **legible** writing. A scrawly squiggle will not do unless there is a 'translation'.

PURCHASE ORDER

The Bed Centre of Town
16 Bedlington Street
Bedford
LU6 2YY

Order No: 013807

Date: 16.05.97

Invoice to:
Director of Finance
Coat of Arms Hotel
Wellingborough
Northants, NN8 6AB

Deliver to:
Director of Finance
Coat of Arms Hotel
Wellingborough
Northants, NN8 6AB

Description	Quantity	Unit Cost	Total
Kingsize Bed	2	784	1,568

Authoriser	Colin Coates	Total Goods	1,568
		VAT	274.40
		Grand Total	**1,842.40**

Signature: VAT Registration No: 641-7701-22

Conditions of Supply:

1 Acceptance of this order implies acceptance of our conditions and terms.
2 All goods and services must be supplied at the prices stated, unless otherwise agreed in writing.
3 All goods must be supplied carriage paid to the delivery point stated above.
4 We reserve the right to reject any goods not in accordance with our description or specification and return the rejected items to the supplier at his cost.
5 Property and risk of the goods shall remain with the supplier until they are delivered at the point specified on the Purchase Order.
6 Time is of the essence with this order and any goods not delivered or services not provided by the delivery date stated may be subject to cancellation.
7 All invoices must quote Purchase Order number.

Figure 1.3 *Purchase Order*

Purchase Orders in larger organisations will usually be quadruplicate copies where the distribution will be as follows:

- top copy (original) to supplier;
- copy to department who ordered the goods;
- copy to Goods Inwards (Stores), Delivery Bay and so on;
- Purchasing Office will retain a copy for files usually in chronological (date order) or numerical order.

Where purchasing is done on a regular basis from suppliers such as brewers, butchers, fishmongers and greengrocers it may not always be possible to raise an official Purchase Order and send it to the supplier as this may take valuable time which, because of the time lag, may cause the client/organisation to run out of stock!

Where this is the case suppliers, as an added service, make regular sales calls, perhaps 2 or 3 times a week, for delivery next day. Where this is the case, the invoice becomes the first piece of official paper, but an 'order book' is normally kept by the purchaser to ensure that what was ordered is what was received.

As all drinks prices have been previously negotiated and you, the purchaser, have decided on quantities, the system works well in practice, if not totally 'by the book' in theory!

Where butcher meat, fish, fruit and vegetables are being ordered, prices can fluctuate on a daily basis. Where this is the case, you are relying on your supplier to keep you informed if prices rise suddenly and, where appropriate, to offer you the customer some alternatives.

Although less common now than it used to be, some à la carte menus have the letters PV beside, for example, lobster or Dover Sole. PV means *Prix variès* in French (price varies), so that the price to the customer differs each day so that the gross profit percentage remained constant. This has largely been replaced nowadays by the daily specials (usually individually priced) which one sees on the blackboard in many restaurants in much the same way as we have guest ales in our pubs.

The moral here is that where food (menus) is concerned, you should be changing your menu at least four times per year if you are unable to negotiate prices for more than 3 months at a time, or you should allow some latitude in your gross profit margin for price changes.

In today's world of electronic communications, orders can be made and acknowledged by fax, via electronic mail (e-mail) and now increasingly via the internet on the world wide web. A printer attached to a computer using electronic means of ordering will satisfy those who prefer a 'hard copy' for their files! When the supplier dispatches the goods, a Delivery Note accompanies the goods.

When the goods are received by the purchaser, they are checked, usually with the Purchase Order. When the supplier sends an invoice, this is 'married up' with the Delivery Note and passed for payment according to your specific payment system. More of this and the remainder of the purchasing cycle in Chapter 3, Recording and controlling the movement of stock.

The Six Principles of Purchasing

1 **Personnel** – who is responsible for purchasing;
2 **Prescription** – quantity/quality and description of goods;
3 **Performance** – of your suppliers in terms of efficiency;
4 **Price** – the best price, given the suitability of the product(s);
5 **Preservation** – effective and efficient storage systems for purchases held in stock prior to re-sale;
6 **Paperwork** – from purchase specification to payment, and all functions in between.

Purchasing is, in fact, a planning exercise, which once in place only needs regular monitoring to keep it feeding efficiently into your business.

Let's take a closer look at the Six Principles of Purchasing:

PERSONNEL

The Purchasing Department
Purchasing Manager
Chef
Owner

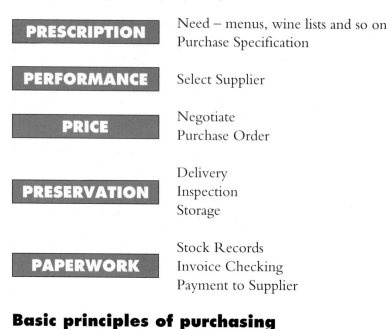

PRESCRIPTION — Need – menus, wine lists and so on
Purchase Specification

PERFORMANCE — Select Supplier

PRICE — Negotiate
Purchase Order

PRESERVATION — Delivery
Inspection
Storage

PAPERWORK — Stock Records
Invoice Checking
Payment to Supplier

Basic principles of purchasing

If you are a small hotel, guest house or bed and breakfast, the 'buying' or 'purchasing' for the business will be part of the owner's or part of one employee's job. In a large organisation, such as a national hotel chain, there may well be a team of people whose sole job is to source and negotiate purchases for the unit(s). Regardless of the size and scale of the purchasing function, the basic purchasing principles will remain the same.

An International Airline Company recently advertised for a Strategic Purchasing Executive. The advertisement which appeared shows just how sophisticated purchasing has become in the larger companies.

STRATEGIC PURCHASING EXECUTIVE

Since the creation of the Airline Purchasing Department, a new approach has been introduced to acquire goods and services and to pro-actively manage the airline's large supply base.

As the Strategic Purchasing Executive – Catering, your specific responsibilities are to:

■ develop supply strategies in conjunction with Inflight Services Department for all catering commodities and services

- manage major contractual relationships with catering service suppliers by working closely with the Strategic Purchasing Manager and senior management of Inflight Services Department
- develop competitive global contracts with a limited number of strategic catering service suppliers
- obtain best value through high level negotiation using market intelligence and more conventional means
- evaluate the potential for upgrading and expanding the supplier base by continuously seeking improvements from current suppliers and encouraging the development of new suppliers as required
- developing creative and innovative approaches to the market which deliver maximum value for the company, minimise risk and exposure and give the company the flexibility required to achieve its business needs

Ideally, you should have:

- tertiary education with emphasis on business or catering
- minimum 5 years' relevant experience, extensive knowledge of airline catering would be a distinct advantage
- exposure to purchasing/contractual/commercial experience
- polished communication and interpersonal skills
- excellent influencing and negotiation skills
- willing to travel regularly

STUDENT EXERCISE

1 List at least 6 essential details which should be shown on a Purchase Order (P/O).

2 Describe and compare the purchasing considerations for the purchase of coffee for the following 2 catering establishments:

a A 150 cover city centre bistro/café;

b A 20 bedroom country house hotel.

3 List 6 duties of a person with responsibility for purchasing.

4 Identify a system of purchasing that may be used for buying cleaning materials for a college kitchen.

2 Recording and Controlling the Movement of Stock

Stock eats up cash very quickly. It's always easier to buy goods than it is to sell them and there are always some items which sell slowly, if at all.

Since the slow stock items remain, and those stock items which sell have to be replaced with more of the same, your stock tends to get bigger and bigger. If this is not properly controlled, more and more money is tied up in lines which you cannot sell until one day you run out of money to restock with the lines or items that you can sell. Any item purchased but not sold is depriving you of profit, but must be paid for.

In any hospitality business, your stores must be organised. However large or small your operation and however sophisticated your stock control process might be, it should do the following things:

1 Allow you to have items grouped together according to their use.
2 Where appropriate, to stop cross-contamination from one set of goods to another.
3 Ensure that your stock is rotated. In other words, the first into stock is the first out of stock.
4 To be able to have a paper system, or a screen system if on a computer, which will show, at any given time, the exact number of any item of stock in as short a time as possible. Also, a system that will allow you to count your stock as effectively and efficiently as possible during whichever methods of stock taking your organisation adopts.

For any stock control system to work effectively, you must understand the system in your head, that is how the stock moves from the supplier through your organisation and to the point of sale where the customer pays you the money for the goods. If the stock items are controlled or piloted through this process, wherever they may be, then you have an efficient system.

The systems which control your stock will vary considerably depending upon the size of your operation and the amount of information you require your stock system to tell you, but in general a stock control system should do the following for you:

1 record what is in stock;

2 give the details of the particular product line or item;

3 record when that item was received into stock and issued out of stock;

4 give information on minimum and maximum levels of stock and reorder quantities;

5 prove that the system is secure and that your records provide a true picture. If you have 2 crates of bottled lager in stock, and you order 10 more, you have 12 in stock. If 6 crates are then issued to the banqueting bar, then 6 crates should be in the cellar and 6 crates should be in the banqueting bar prior to being sold, or there should be money from sales of beer in the banqueting till. This is the ultimate part of a stock control system which proves its efficiency and effectiveness.

From the moment goods are delivered to your back door, they are costing you money. They are now *your* responsibility.

If they fail to arrive at their designated point of sale (in front of the customer) they are not going to attract the selling price, and therefore the profit you require in order to run a profitable business. Or, if they fail to arrive at the point of sale in a condition that the customer is prepared to pay the agreed price, you may not be able to sell at top price, therefore your profit is eroded.

If you fail to get the goods to the point of sale because they deteriorated or became damaged and had to be discarded, then your profit is eroded because you will have to pay for the goods (unless you can prove that the damage was caused by your supplier or the carrier) but you won't be able to sell them:

Cost of goods	£1.20p
Selling Price	£0.00p
Gross Profit	− **£1.20p**

PROBLEM!

What you need to make sure of is that the goods you buy are controlled and nurtured from the point at which they enter the premises to the point at which they are turned into hard cash – the customers paying their bills.

A successful business is one which has many customers who return again and again for 'more of the same'.

It is without question that part of that business success will be invested in an efficient and effective stock control system.

So let's pick up on what happens to goods when they are delivered to our premises and once again look at the purchasing cycle figure from Chapter 1.

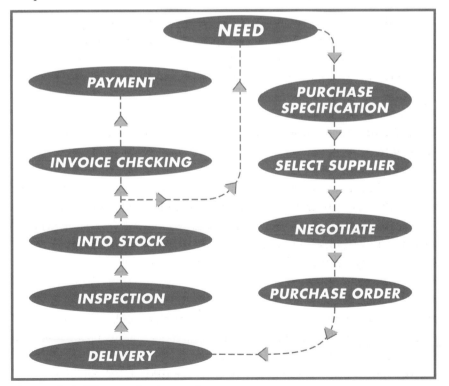

Figure 2.1 *The purchasing cycle*

The purchasing cycle (see Figure 2.1)

- Delivery (arrival on your premises)
- Inspection
- Into stock
- Invoice checking
- Payment

Delivery and inspection

Check the goods, first of all against the Delivery Note, for quantity, and if possible, quality.

A complete check is not always possible. If, for example, 10 cases of frozen chicken arrive, you may not be able to check every box, but you can at least acknowledge that 10 boxes did arrive.

In larger organisations there will be a store clerk or store keeper, part of whose job will be to receive all goods. In a smaller organisation this may well be the chef or the proprietor.

I have been in businesses where, due to a lack of understanding, deliveries are hardly ever checked and signatures hardly ever received. Worst still, I've been in places where people sign for goods without ever checking them!

This can be an expensive practice and is almost inexcusable. Where there is an excuse for not checking goods (the hotel is on fire) then they should be signed for, but with the words 'received unchecked' written on the delivery person's paperwork/goods received book.

In some organisations, details from the Delivery Note (duly checked against the goods) are entered into a Goods Received Book or are written onto a Goods Received Sheet which is sent to the Purchase Department.

If the above system is in operation (that is, a storeman) then he will already have a copy of the P/O sent from the Purchase Department, so he will be able to check that off against the Delivery Note and advise the Purchasing Department of any differences by way of the Goods Received Note.

Goods into stock

If the goods have been inspected and found to be satisfactory, then the goods immediately go **into stock** and **into storage**.

Into stock – the information from the Delivery Note is entered onto your paperwork (or via a computer screen) usually onto a stock card or bin card.

Into storage – the type of store in which the goods are physically kept. This will depend upon the type of goods, for example:
- spirits – in which case they will go to the cellar;
- meats – to the chill or (for example with frozen chicken breasts) to the frozen store;
- fruit and vegetables – to the appropriate store in or near the kitchen;
- tins (for example kidney beans) – into the dry goods store.

Invoice checking and payment

Shortly after receiving the goods, the Accounts Department will receive an invoice (bill) for the goods for which, in due course (4–8 weeks), the supplier will expect payment.

We must, therefore, make sure that all goods received arrive at their appropriate destination. This may be into storage in the chill room, the freezer or the cellar, or it may be that goods are going straight to the kitchen or the bar for 'processing' and therefore immediate selling. If the goods are going immediately to the point of sale, care has to be taken that the information is written up on the storage or bin cards, even though the goods by-pass the storage process.

We need to know at any moment in time, what the balance is of the items which we have in storage, so that we can re-order before we run out.

How many times have you sat down in a café or bistro and chosen from the menu only to be told that the item you have chosen is off the menu? There could be many reasons for this, but if you are operating an efficient stock control system, it shouldn't be because you 'ran out' of stock (not unless you can prove exceptional circumstances (for example an extra 300 guests arrived at a wedding and you didn't expect them!).

So, as soon as goods go into storage a note is made on a stock card or a bin card. This will immediately show the status, that is how many there are of that particular stock item, and will be written in ink or shown on a computer screen.

Whichever way you keep your records (manual or computerised) you physically have to write down (or enter into the computer) the details, so don't think a computer will cut out *all* the work – it won't!

A bin card or a stock card will be written up by the Storekeeper, or whoever is designated in the business to do that job.

A stock or bin card will show the movement of stock and will also show the balance of what is in the store at any given time. Here is an example of one.

STOCK CARD/BIN CARD			
Item = Chicken Supreme 7oz		Minimum Stock 2 × 32	
Date	Receipts	Issues	Balance
4/6/9–	4		4
6/6/9–	–	2	2
18/6/9–	6	–	8
28/6/9–	–	5	3

If we study the stock card/bin card a little more closely, we will see that on 6 June the stores issued 2 boxes of 7oz chicken supremes.

This was on receipt of another piece of paper from the chef called a Stores Requisition, and no goods may leave any of the stores without a Stores or Stock Requisition sheet to support the movement of the stock.

This meant that by the end of the 6 June, the stock of 7oz chicken supremes was down to the minimum level of 2 boxes. This prompted another piece of paper, this time from the Stores to the Purchasing Department, advising the Purchasing Department, or maybe even the chef, if he or she is the authorised purchaser of food, which is very likely, that the stock of that particular item is at minimum level and that more should be ordered in order to avoid the item going 'out of stock'.

Another 6 boxes of chicken were ordered and duly delivered on 18 June which, added to the 2 boxes already in stock, brought the balance up to 8 boxes. Ten days later on 28 June a Stock Requisition Sheet was sent to the stores for 5 boxes of chicken.

The 5 boxes were sent to the kitchen, entered onto the stock card, which left the balance of 3 boxes remaining in the stores.

As the minimum stock level is 2 boxes, and the present balance is 3, we would be wise to re-order now if there is to be short-term demand for chicken supremes.

Let's explain minimum and maximum stock levels and re-order levels in more detail.

Minimum stock levels

This is the amount of stock that is needed for each stock item held, bearing in mind operational need (demand) and suppliers' delivery periods.

Demand × delivery period = minimum stock

4 boxes per week × 3 days (3/7 week) = 1.71 (say 2 boxes)

If you were only able to have deliveries say, every two weeks, the minimum stock carried would be 8:

Demand × delivery period = minimum stock

4 boxes per week × 2 weeks = 8 minimum stock

Re-order level of stock

Because of the risks involved in relying on prompt deliveries, a figure for extra stock (often 25% of minimum stock) is added to the minimum stock.

This level of stock is the trigger to go ahead and purchase a new supply of goods, and where this information is held on computer, some computer programmes will automatically re-order by printing a purchase order or will automatically warn you to re-order by visual means (perhaps a flashing item on screen).

The re-order formula is as follows:

Minimum stock + 25% extra stock = re-order level

4 boxes + 1 box = 5 boxes

Maximum stock level

When establishing the maximum level of stock that can be held, the actual physical capacity of your storage facilities will have to be taken into consideration.

In addition, it is good practice to keep your stock levels lower rather than higher. This keeps the money in the bank and not tied up in the store room for months on end. There is no point in carrying 4 months' stock of an item if you can order the item weekly or monthly at no extra cost.

Stock taking

The purpose of a stock take is to check the actual physical stock held, against the various stores records (bin cards, stock cards, and so on) and to verify that the information from the paperwork has been accurately transcribed, and tallies with the physical goods in stock. For example, if the bin card for gin (the gin-bin!) indicates that there are 23 × litre bottles of gin in the cellar, it is important to check that there actually are 23 litre bottles of gin awaiting movement to the bars for consumption.

Stock taking also allows for the valuation (£) of current stock holding to be done which, in turn, will provide data which will contribute to the bar or food stock results.

A stock take is always taken at the end of your financial year for the purposes of valuing the stock that you have for your balance sheet (see Chapter 13).

However, stock taking should be done more often than once per year in order to ensure that you are not carrying too much stock, and so that if there are discrepancies between what you think you have in stock and what you actually have in stock, you don't have to wait 12 months to find out.

As well as period stock taking as above, the on-going or continuous stock taking method, or the random stock taking method, can also be utilised.

On-going/continuous stock taking

This involves stock being continuously physically checked so that each stock item is verified at least once a year.

The system should be devised so that a number of stock items are checked on every working day, with valuable or fast moving items being checked more often.

Random stock taking

This type of stock taking involves selecting a number of stock items at random. A stock take is then carried out on those items and the results recorded.

With this method staff will not be aware which items have been selected for stock taking, which would reduce potential pilferage, and comparisons of results with the stock records will indicate the efficiency of your operation without the need for a full stock take.

In larger establishments external specialist stock takers are employed on a contract to carry out regular stock takes (or inventories, as they are sometimes known).

As one of the main reasons for stock taking is to put monetary value on the stock held, it is important to use either the valuation of the last batch of any items going into stock (LIFO) or the first item going into stock (FIFO) where LIFO is Last In First Out and FIFO is First In First Out.

Apart from the obvious problems of food and drink items going past their 'sell-by' dates, thus obviating the use of First In First Out, using a combination of the two methods will produce inconsistencies in the stock valuations, so only one method should be chosen.

STUDENT EXERCISE

1 Identify 5 pieces of information which an efficient stock control system should tell you.

2 What is the purpose of a bin card?

3 Complete the following bin card, using the undernoted information and show the balance as at 21 October.

Bin No: 324	Item:	Tuna Chunks in Oil
Max Stock: 120	Unit Size: 800g	
	Min Stock: 24	

Date	Received	Issued	Balance
1/10			26

On 3 October 12 × 800g Tuna Chunks were issued
On 4 October 48 × 800g Tuna Chunks were received
On 9 October 16 × 800g Tuna Chunks were issued
On 16 October 18 × 500g Tuna Chunks were issued
On 20 October 6 × 800g Tuna Chunks were issued
On 21 October 36 × 800g Tuna Chunks were received.

4 Identify and compare three different methods of stock taking which may be used to verify the accuracy of your stock records.

5 Why should stock taking take place more often than once per year?

3 Storage and the Law/ Storage for Profit

As we have seen from the previous chapter, a lot of time, effort and planning has gone into purchasing goods and services for the hospitality business.

As soon as any of the commodities purchased arrive at our service door, they become the responsibility of the unit, therefore a highly responsible approach has to be taken to the storage of the various goods that we buy in prior to and during the time which we 'manufacture' the goods to the end product – the food and drink consumed by our customers.

Once again, we have many factors to consider when looking at the storage systems for our goods. Obviously different goods require different storage conditions and we will look at these in this chapter.

As responsible managers in the hospitality industry, the following will have to be taken into consideration when dealing with storage of goods:

1 Food Safety Act, 1990;
2 Food Safety Regulations, 1995;
3 Health and Safety at Work Act (HASAWA), 1974.

Where storage conditions are inadequate for goods purchased, money will be wasted. This wastage will manifest itself in a significant drop in Gross Profit (GP). Goods may deteriorate, which means they will be unfit for human consumption. This will affect our gross profit margin, because goods have been bought in (purchases) but have not become sales as they have had to be thrown out. In addition, inadequate storage conditions may cause at best stomach upset, and at worst acute food poisoning, which will obviously affect sales immediately and then far into the future.

The main food hygiene regulations of importance in the hospitality industry are:

1 Food Safety (general food hygiene) Regulations, 1995;
2 Food Hygiene (temperature control) Regulations, 1995.

These regulations place a strong emphasis on owners and managers to identify safety risks and to design and implement appropriate preventive measures which may include Hazard Analysis and Critical Control Points (HACCP) and/or Assured Safe Catering (ASC) which will be described in greater depth later on in this chapter.

Food Safety (general food hygiene) Regulations, 1995

These regulations place two general requirements on owners and managers in the hospitality industry, amongst others:

1 to ensure that all food handling operations are carried out hygienically and in accordance with the rules of hygiene;
2 to identify and control all potential food safety hazards, which will involve a systematic approach such as HACCP or ASC.

The Food Safety (general food hygiene) Regulations, 1995 are contained in 10 chapters which cover:

■ Food Premises
■ Food Rooms
■ Moveable Premises including marquees, market stalls, mobile vehicles and vending machines
■ Transport
■ Equipment
■ Food Waste
■ Water supplies
■ Personal Hygiene
■ Food stuffs
■ Training

Food Safety (temperature control) Regulations, 1995

These regulations came into force on 15 September 1995 and replace earlier and more complex regulations. There are now only two important temperatures: 8 degrees centigrade, 63 degrees centigrade (plus 82 degrees centigrade in Scotland).

Foods which may be subject to 'microbiological multiplication' must be held at no more than 8 degrees centigrade or above 63 degrees centigrade. There are a few exceptions which include food on display, which can be displayed for up to 4 hours and also low risk and preserve food which can be stored at an ambient temperature.

Food which is to be served hot should be held at over 63 degrees centigrade. Food reheated in Scotland must attain a temperature of 82 degrees centigrade, unless this will adversely affect the food.

Hazard Analysis and Critical Control Points (HACCP)

HACCP is a preventive quality control system. This approach to food safety is based on a systematic analysis of all hazards or risks involved in buying, receiving, storing, producing and serving food. All possible hazards are identified and the likelihood of them happening is assessed. Certain foods pose certain risks at particular stages in the process. These risks are identified and measures are then designed to control and eliminate the risk of hazard.

Recommended shelf lives

Cooked foods, frozen foods, ice cream, cheeses, dairy foods, fish, meat products, cooked and raw meat and poultry, require adequate storage conditions which will be different in each case. Furthermore, canned foods, dried foods and bottled goods will also require adequate storage conditions. Where manufacturers recommend 'use by' dates, these should also be adhered to.

For further information on this, please refer to *Croner's Catering*.

In more simple terms, as goods arrive at the back door for delivery, they pass along four main channels:

■ dry goods go to the Dry Goods Store;
■ vegetables and grocery products go to the Fridge or the Vegetable Store;
■ frozen foods go to the Freezer;
■ fresh perishable products go to the Cold Rooms or Chill Rooms.

The type of operation will dictate the storage conditions and the proportion of those conditions in the preparation rooms, that is fast food operations will use more frozen products, and will rely more on freezers than on refrigerators. An up-market restaurant on the other hand may need much more space for fresh vegetables and perishable goods which will require refrigeration rather than freezing.

It is now worth noting that the storage of waste products from the hospitality industry, prior to disposal, needs to be considered. The Environmental Protection Act 1990 imposes a 'duty of care' on anyone who produces or disposes of 'controlled' waste. So far as the hospitality industry is concerned the effect of the Act is to ensure that all waste is stored correctly and disposed of correctly. All waste holders (which includes the hospitality industry) must act to keep waste safe against:

■ corrosion of ware of the waste containers;
■ accidental spilling or leaking, whether caused by accident, the weather and scavenging by animals or people.

In addition, the new Land Fill Tax which was introduced at the end of 1996 will cost all waste producers a minimum of £7 per tonne, in addition to any other disposal costs they may have at present.

Health and Safety at Work Act, 1974

This legislation covers storage in as much as lifting procedures from storage areas need to be considered. This will prevent serious injury or worse. Typical tasks which need to be addressed in the hospitality industry include:

■ lifting kegs and barrels from delivery position to cellars or bar areas;
■ lifting gas cylinders and crates of bottles on delivery and re-stocking shelves;

■ also the storage of boxes of post-mix syrups and the handling of bottle skips or bins.

In the housekeeping department the storage of clean and dirty linen and the storage of bags of wet towels and bath mats needs to be risk assessed under the Health and Safety at Work Act.

In the kitchen the movement of waste food bins and other waste receptacles, the lifting position of dishwasher chemicals and containers and the loading and unloading of storage trays in the dishwasher need to be considered, as do sacks of fruit and vegetables and boxes of frozen food.

The law also requires that we control hazardous substances in the storage and use of chemicals. This is under the Control of Substances Hazardous to Health Regulations, 1994 (COSHH). Where chemicals and substances are stored a risk assessment must be made, for example cleaning chemicals including alkalis and acids, detergents, sanitisers and descalers. Also burnishing chemicals and machine oils in the kitchen. In the bar, beer type or line cleaner, glass washing detergent and sanitisers need to be stored correctly, as do polishes and fuel for flambé lamps, be it LPG or methylated spirits.

Where hotels have leisure facilities, then water treatment chemicals need also come under this legislation, for instance where swimming pools are concerned.

Storage for profit

Having looked at the legal aspect of storage, let us now spend some time looking at the profit aspect of storage.

Wherever goods are stored, and in whatever condition, it is vitally important that wastage (for whatever reason) is kept to a minimum. Wastage will occur for the following reasons:
■ goods go past their sell-by date;
■ goods are damaged through careless storage;
■ theft and pilferage.

Old stock should always be brought to the front of the shelf in any storage facility. This minimises the risk of goods going past sell-by dates and thus minimises the risk of the purchased goods not attracting profit. It is also important that goods are stored securely against the risk of theft or pilferage. In subsequent chapters we will look at the paperwork which will expose such action, but prevention is the main name of the game. By removing the opportunity for people to steal, the risk is greatly minimised. This means that all storage areas, including fridges, chill rooms and freezers should have a lock which should be used and keys to those locks should be held by responsible members of staff. Duplicate keys should be few and all should be accounted for. Access should be restricted to key holders only, and the appropriate paperwork actioned at every opportunity.

If, for whatever reason, wastage occurs in the food or beverage operation of a hospitality business, the results can be as follows.

Let us assume that purchases of £400 will produce sales of £1000. If 10% of the purchases are wasted for whatever reason, let's say £40 worth of purchases, then they will not produce the attached proportion of profit of the selling price which, in this case, is £100. This means that sales are only £900, but purchases are still £400 because it is unlikely you can go back to any supplier and say 'please give me a credit for the food I wasted because my fridge was not up to temperature'. Your supplier is unlikely to take this responsibility because it's yours, so consequently the purchases remain at £400, but as the sales are £900 and not £1000, your profit is £500 and not £600.

Purchase Price	Selling Price	Gross Profit
£400	£1000	£600
After 10% loss of goods purchased but not sold:		
£400 Still have to pay	£900 (Selling Price reduced by £100)	£500 (£100 less Profit)

This has a significant effect on the percentage profit which you make and this will be illustrated further in Chapter 13.

STUDENT EXERCISE

1 Explain the different storage conditions that may be required for the kitchen of a 50 bedroom hotel with a 100 cover family restaurant attached.

2 Explain how the Health and Safety at Work Act, 1974 applies in catering storage areas.

4
Making Your Calculator Work for You

As I go about my daily business of helping people to set up new ventures and helping existing businesses to become more competitive, I often come across people who have a total mental block when it comes to figures. The minute you mention percentages and ratios, the door slams and footsteps are heard running down the corridor.

They somehow believe that you have to be a qualified accountant in order to understand words like margins, mark-ups, net and gross profits, profit and loss accounts and balance sheets.

What you need to know in order to understand about costing and purchasing and the control of profits in the hospitality industry is:
■ basic arithmetic;
■ basic calculator skills.

The latter does not involve buying or using a calculator which will get you to the moon and back, or one which allows you to find the square root of anything at the touch of a button. What you do need is to be able to know the difference between £1, 10p and 1p when entering such figures into a calculator, and knowing how to use the plus (+), minus (−), multiplication (×), division (÷), percentages (%) and equals (=) buttons on a calculator.

For the purposes of this book forget the rest apart, of course, from digits 0–9.

As we said earlier, you also need to know basic arithmetic, such as

100 minus 40 = 60.

You do also need to understand the principles of profit, outlined below.

1 Sell the product to your customer for more than you paid for it!

2 Sell the product to attract enough profit in order for you to pay for your labour.

3 Sell the product to attract enough profit in order for you to pay for your labour, plus your expenses such as rent, rates, electricity or motor expenses.

4 Sell the product so that after you deduct all your expenses, you make a profit at the end of the year which is greater than you would receive if all you did with the money invested in your business was deposit it in the bank.

This last point can be further explained.

If you won the lottery and decided to buy an hotel for £750 000, you ought to make more at the end of the year than you would have if you invested the £750 000 in the Building Society or Bank.

Let's say that at present you will get an interest rate (return) of 7% on your money. At the end of the year you will have £750 000 × 7% = £52 500 for doing **absolutely nothing**. Unless you can steer your hotel in which you have invested £750 000, to a profit before tax of at least £52 500 why bother? Because to do so will involve a lot of work and effort.

However, if this work and effort is channelled in the right direction and planned from the start, you can make considerably more than 7% return on your capital, **so read on**.

First of all, let's confirm that we all know how to use our calculators properly. Let's look at the problems which we may encounter which can distort our answers.

When I run training courses for aspects of costing and purchasing for the hospitality industry, I inevitably have people who beat their calculators and throw them around the room because they (the calculators) have given the 'wrong answer'. However, it is usually the information put into the calculator which is wrong!

Alternatively, training course delegates tell me that they find it easier to calculate using either mental arithmetic or by using the ancient art of 'long division'. This I admire greatly, and we move along happily until I ask the delegates to calculate 63.93% of £248 964.

At this point, I dissuade those who are using the mental arithmetic approach from leaving (because they have a headache), and suggest that even with a time limit of 1 hour (and it is rare that such time is available) those toiling with the long division approach may not succeed.

It is at this point that we should run through a few calculator exercises just to remind ourselves of decimal points, significant figures, rounding up, and so on.

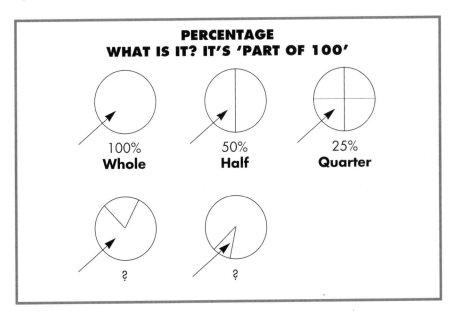

Figure 4.1 *To calculate less obvious percentages we need to use our calculators*

If £1 = 100 pennies, then 1p is $\dfrac{1}{100}$ of a £1, 44p is $\dfrac{44}{100}$ of a £1, and 100p = $\dfrac{100}{100}$ of a £1 and that equals £1.

Question Can you put a £1 into a calculator without using a screw-driver?

Answer Yes

Putting a £1.00 into a calculator is easy	1.0
Now put £1.10 into your calculator	1.10
Now put 10p into your calculator	.10
Now put 1p into your calculator	.01
Now put 5p into your calculator	.05
Now put 50p into your calculator	.50
Now put 1p again into your calculator	0.01

i.e., .5 = 50p, .05 = 5p

Now put £1.50 into your calculator	1.50

Question: What is 50% of £1.50?

Answer: It's half of £1.50, which is 75p – we can all do that in our head

Now do that in your calculator

$1.50 \times 50\% = 0.75$

Get your calculator brain in gear

Before starting any calculations, hit the $\boxed{\textbf{AC}}$ (All Clear) button. This will clear the calculator of all previous calculations. Then try these:

$54 + 124 - 64 \quad = 114$

$963 \times (42 - 56) = -13\,482$

To do this calculation, you must first do the calculation in brackets, then multiply it by 963.

$42 - 56 \qquad = -14$

$963 \times (-14) \qquad = -13\,482$

Very often figures which are preceded by a minus, such as $-13\,482$, will be shown in brackets. This is standard practice when, for example, such a figure shows up as a loss in accounts.

123456 × 654321 = E807.79853

By pressing the [C] button, the E will disappear, but this calculation has seriously overloaded your calculator.

Now hit the [AC] button and the calculator will return to 0, which is the idle position.

Now let's try a few percentages.

Question: What is 10% of 1500?

On the calculator this is done as follows:

1500 × 10%

Answer: 150

You will note that in this case you don't have to press the equals [=] button, but if you do, the answer remains the same.

Question: What does a 20% discount on 500 give us?

On the calculator this is done as follows:

500 × 20% = 100

Answer: 500 − 100 = 400

In this example, the calculator calculates that 20% of 500 is 100 and when you hit the minus [−] button, the 100 is deducted from the 500 to give the correct answer of 400.

Look how easy it now is to find 63.93% of £248 964.00. The calculation is as follows:

£248 964.00 × 63.93%

Answer: £159 162.68

When we arrive at an answer which includes pence (pennies!) as well as pounds, we may choose to round up or round down according to the scale of the calculations.

In this case, we have 68 pence which, because the 8 is nearer to 10 than 0, you may wish to round up to 70p.

Alternatively, you may wish to round up to the next nearest pound which, in this case, would be £159 163 (if you wanted to do away with the pence calculations altogether).

It can become very tedious when you are inputting large sums into a calculator to constantly have extra figures after the decimal point. This is why, at the beginning of such an exercise, we often do away with the pence altogether.

This would obviously not be the case if we were calculating smaller sums made up of pence, for instance the cost of a portion of chips. We would obviously be very interested in knowing the pennies as well as the pounds, as a portion of chips is much less expensive, therefore more price sensitive than, say, the total sales for all Burger King restaurants in the UK.

Recommended reading

Calculations for Hospitality and Catering, Gordon E. Gee (Hodder and Stoughton).

5
Margins and
Mark-Ups

An Englishman, an Irishman and a Scotsman were having a drink at a Catering Conference in the Scotsman's hotel. They started to discuss business and inevitably they got onto the subject of profitability. The question they wanted answered was, who was the most successful caterer, given that their **net profits** were as follows:

- Englishman   £60 000
- Irishman   £19 000
- Scotsman   £38 000

So, who *was* most successful?

We can't answer the question from the information given, because what we need to know is what percentage of sales that profit represents. Once we know that, we can compare the business results of the Englishman, the Irishman and the Scotsman in a more meaningful way.

So let's find out what the **sales** or **turnover** is for each of the businesses.
- Englishman's sales   £400 000
- Irishman's sales   £130 000
- Scotsman's sales   £250 000

The most obvious conclusion to come to is that the Englishman is the most successful businessman because his profit is the largest. But when we measure profit in a business, we are measuring efficiency, and the more efficient you are, the more profit you will squeeze out of your sales or turnover.

So let's see what **percentage profit** each operator has squeezed out of their business by comparing like with like and dividing the net profit by the turnover in each case and multiplying by 100.

$$\boxed{\text{Net profit \% = net profit} \div \text{turnover} \times 100}$$

Thus, the calculations are as follows:

Englishman $\dfrac{60\ 000}{400\ 000} \times 100 = 15\%$

Irishman $\dfrac{19\ 000}{130\ 000} \times 100 = 14.6\%$

Scotsman $\dfrac{38\ 000}{250\ 000} \times 100 = 15.2\%$

The net profits of between 14.6% and 15.2% compare favourably with the 7% which you may attract as a return on your money if invested in the Bank or Building Society.

They all reckoned they were fairly successful, so they had another drink. After further discussions, they wondered why the Scotsman was just that slight percentage higher on net profit.

'Well', he said, 'I control my operation very tightly, and by the way, you owe me £13.50p for the last two rounds of drinks!'

Let's now make sure we are clear about margins and mark-ups as they apply in the hospitality business.

First of all let's look at the difference between a **Gross Profit Margin** and a **mark-up**. It is vitally important that you know the difference.

Gross Profit Margin is the gross profit (GP) expressed as a percentage of the selling price (SP). For example:

$$GP\% = \dfrac{GP}{SP} \times 100$$

Example: If the selling price is £3.95p (excluding VAT) and the food cost has been calculated at £1.50p, what Gross Profit Percentage (GP%) has been achieved?

If the selling price is £3.95p and the food cost (FC) is £1.50p, the gross profit is the difference between the two: £3.95 − £1.50 = £2.45

$$GP\% = \frac{2.45}{3.95} \times 100 = 62\%$$

Mark-up: The mark-up gives the gross profit as a percentage of the cost, for example:

$$\text{Mark up} = \frac{GP}{FC} \times 100$$

In the above example, this would produce a mark-up of:

$$\text{Mark up} = \frac{2.45}{1.50} \times 100 = 163\%$$

Let's calculate a few more examples:

Food Cost		Selling Price		Gross Profit
40p		£1.00		60p
GP%	=	$\frac{GP}{SP} \times 100$		
GP%	=	$\frac{0.60}{1.00} \times 100$	=	60%
Mark-up	=	$\frac{GP}{FC} \times 100$		
Mark-up	=	$\frac{0.60}{0.40} \times 100$	=	150%

Food Cost		Selling Price	Gross Profit
80p		£3.40	£2.60
GP%	=	$\frac{GP}{SP} \times 100$ i.e.,	$\frac{2.60}{3.40} \times 100 = 76.47\%$
Mark-up	=	$\frac{GP}{FC} \times 100$ i.e.,	$\frac{2.60}{0.80} \times 100 = 325\%$

Food Cost	**Selling Price**	**Gross Profit**
72p	£1.33	61p

$$\text{GP\%} = \frac{GP}{SP} \times 100 \text{ i.e.,} \quad \frac{0.61}{1.33} \times 100 = 45.86\%$$

$$\text{Mark-up} = \frac{GP}{FC} \times 100 \text{ i.e.,} \quad \frac{0.61}{0.72} \times 100 = 84.72\%$$

Food Cost	**Selling Price**	**Gross Profit**
£1.50	£2.25	75p

$$\text{GP\%} = \frac{GP}{SP} \times 100 \text{ i.e.,} \quad \frac{0.75}{2.25} \times 100 = 33.33\%$$

$$\text{Mark-up} = \frac{GP}{FC} \times 100 \text{ i.e.,} \quad \frac{0.75}{1.50} \times 100 = 50\%$$

Food Cost	**Selling Price**	**Gross Profit**
£2.80	£4.48	£1.68

$$\text{GP\%} = \frac{GP}{SP} \times 100 \text{ i.e.,} \quad \frac{1.68}{4.48} \times 100 = 37.5\%$$

$$\text{Mark-up} = \frac{GP}{FC} \times 100 \text{ i.e.,} \quad \frac{1.68}{2.80} \times 100 = 60\%$$

If we put this into tabular form, it looks like this:

Food Cost	= FC
Selling Price	= SP
Gross Profit	= GP
Gross Profit %	= GP%
Mark-up	= Mark-up

FC	SP	GP	GP%	Mark-up
40p	£1.00	60p	60%	150%
80p	£3.40	£2.60	76.47%	325%
72p	£1.33	61p	45.86%	85%
£1.50	£2.25	75p	33.33%	50%
£2.80	£4.48	£1.68	37.5%	60%

Here's a thought. If you buy a pie for 50p and sell it for £1, what is your gross profit margin and what is your mark-up?

Answer: $\quad$ GP% $\quad = \dfrac{GP}{SP} \times 100 = \dfrac{50p}{1.00} \times 100 = 50\%$

$$\text{Mark-up} = \dfrac{GP}{FC} \times 100 = \dfrac{50p}{50p} \times 100 = 100\%$$

A Ready Reckoner which converts margins to mark-ups is contained in the Glossary at the back of this book.

One of my favourite exercises involves the costing and pricing of half a Galia melon.

Let's assume that you halve the melon. Place on a doiley, and onto an entrée plate/coupe/or whatever and serve garnished with two fresh cherries and some fresh mint leaves at the side.

The food cost obviously depends upon the season as Galia melon can vary in price over the year, but let's say that the half melon cost 30p, and the cherries and mint leaves for garnish another 2p.

Let's assume that we wish to apply a Gross Profit of 65%, which would be highly acceptable (given the industry norm of approximately 58% to 70%). At what price must we sell the melon in order to achieve this?

The formula is as follows:

$$\text{Selling Price} = \dfrac{FC}{FC\%} \times 100$$

Remember that the GP% and the FC% **must** add up to 100%.

Therefore, if we require a GP% of 65%, the FC% must be 35%.

$$\text{Selling Price} = \frac{0.32}{35} \times 100 = 0.91428$$

It is incredible how often people produce an answer of £91.42p or £9.14p when, in fact, the correct answer is 91.42p (call it 92p).

What you must make sure of is using the decimal point in the correct place when putting the figures into your calculator.

If you input 15 instead of 0.15, the answer will be as follows:

$$\frac{15}{35} \times 100 = 42.85$$

If you input 1.5 instead of 0.15, the answer will be as follows:

$$\frac{1.5}{35} \times 100 = 4.28$$

Why? Because when you put 15 into a calculator, you are inputting £15.

So, if the cost of your food is £15 and you require a Gross Profit Margin of 65%, the answer will be greater than £15 and is, in fact, £42.85p.

When you put 1.5 into a calculator you are inputting £1.50.

So, if the cost of your food is £1.50p and you require a Gross Profit Margin of 65%, the answer will be greater than £1.50p and is, in fact £4.28p.

So, when you put 0.15 into a calculator, you are inputting 15p and the correct answer is 0.428p (call it 43p).

So, when you are calculating the costs and subsequently the selling prices of your menus or menu items, step back for a moment and look at it from the 'common sense' pricing point of view.

Perhaps £9.14 is a lot to charge for half a melon!

The sales mix

Hotel sales are made up of 3 distinctive elements:
- room sales;
- food sales;
- beverage sales.

It is vitally important that you know what proportion of your total sales each one of the above components represents, and you need to constantly monitor this mix of sales.

You need to know your sales mix for two reasons:

1 You need to compare figures from one period to the other in order to react to any trends which may be showing.

2 You need also to know your sales mix in order to calculate how efficient each department is in its pursuit of laid down departmental Gross Profit targets.

We will study **1** first.

The formula for calculating the sales mix is:

Departmental Sales divided by Total Sales × 100, that is

$$\frac{\text{Department Sales}}{\text{Total Sales}} \times 100$$

Calculating sales mix

Total Sales of an hotel for Year 6 of trading are £1 200 000, made up of the following:

Rooms	£ 446 000
Food	£ 425 000
Beverage	£ 291 000
Other	£ 38 000
	£1 200 000

The sales mix is as follows:

Rooms $\dfrac{446\ 000}{1\ 200\ 000} \times 100 = 37.2\%$

Food $\dfrac{425\ 000}{1\ 200\ 000} \times 100 = 35.4\%$

Beverage $\dfrac{291\ 000}{1\ 200\ 000} \times 100 = 24.2\%$

Other $\dfrac{38\ 000}{1\ 200\ 000} \times 100 = 3.2\%$

This will allow us to compare our departmental sales, year on year, month on month or week on week.

Let's compare the above figures with the figures for the same hotel the following year.

Year 7 Figures

Total Sales	1 220 000
Rooms	455 000
Food	397 000
Beverage	285 000
Other	83 000

The sales mix is as follows:

Rooms $\dfrac{455\ 000}{1\ 220\ 000} \times 100 = 37.3\%$

Food $\dfrac{397\ 000}{1\ 220\ 000} \times 100 = 32.5\%$

Beverage $\dfrac{285\ 000}{1\ 220\ 000} \times 100 = 23.4\%$

Other $\dfrac{83\ 000}{1\ 220\ 000} \times 100 = 6.8\%$

	Year 6	% Sales Mix	Year 7	% Sales Mix	
Total	1 200 000		1 220 000		+£20 000
Rooms	446 000	37.3%	455 000	37.3%	+£9 000
Food	425 000	35.4%	397 000	32.5%	−£28 000
Beverage	291 000	24.2%	285 000	23.4%	−£6 000
Other	38 000	3.2%	83 000	6.8%	+£45 000

Turnover is up by £20 000 from £1 200 000 to £1 220 000 and if it was only the total turnover figures that you were presented with, you would be none the wiser!

However, by comparing the sales mix from one year to another, we are able to establish that there has been a shift in the pattern of sales as seen in the box above.

This needs some explanation from the Unit Manager, and it is as follows:

Food and beverage sales declined (food down from £425 000 to £397 000 and beverage down from £291 000 to £285 000) because of increased competition from new additions to the market.

There was, however, a slight compensation by a marginal increase in accommodation income (up £9000 from £446 000 to £455 000).

However, it was because of the new leisure facility that had come on stream in Year 7 (Other, up £45 000 from £38 000 to £83 000) that there was an overall increase in total revenue for the business.

Sales mix and overall Gross Profit

Let's now look at sales mix in relation to the overall Gross Profit of the hotel. In other words, how effective was each of the departments in contributing to the overall Gross Profit of the hotel.

Let's say that Gross Profit margins have been set as follows:

Rooms   100%
Food   65%
Beverage 60%

Let's now look at our hotel for Years 6 and 7 and see what difference the sales mix has made to our Gross Profit, assuming that we achieve the required cost of Sales/Gross Profit targets.

Year 6 – Departmental Sales

Year 6	Sales	Sales Mix
Rooms	446 000	37.2%
Food	425 000	35.4%
Beverage	291 000	24.2%

Gross Profit for each Department

	Sales	Required GP Margin	Gross Profit
Rooms	446 000 ×	100% =	446 000
Food	425 000 ×	65% =	276 250
Beverage	291 000 ×	60% =	174 600
	£1 162 000	Overall GP =	**£896 850**

With the shift in sales mix for Year 7, the figures are as follows:

Year 7	Sales	Sales Mix
Rooms	455 000	37.3%
Food	397 000	32.5%
Beverage	285 000	23.4%

Gross Profit for each Department

	Sales	Required GP Margin	Gross Profit
Rooms	455 000 ×	100% =	455 000
Food	397 000 ×	65% =	258 050
Beverage	285 000 ×	60% =	171 000
	1 137 000		**£884 050**

So, the difference in total sales is £25 000 down from Year 6 to Year 7.

The total Gross Profit percentage achieved in each year is as follows:

Year 6, Gross Profit = 896 850 on Sales of 1 162 000

$$\text{Overall Gross Profit percentage is } \frac{896\ 850}{1\ 162\ 000} \times 100 = 77.18\%$$

Year 7, Gross Profit = 884 050 on Sales of 1 137 000

$$\text{Overall Gross Profit percentage is } \frac{884\ 050}{1\ 137\ 000} \times 100 = 77.75\%$$

So, here we have some interesting figures.

1 Total Sales for the 3 departments in Year 7 are down £25 000 (1 162 000 to 1 137 000).

2 Total Gross Profit in Year 7 is down £12 800 (896 850 to 884 050).

3 The overall Gross Profit margin is up from 77.18% in Year 6 to 77.75% in Year 7.

Let's look further at the importance of Turnover (sales), Gross Profit and the Gross Profit % in relation to sales mix.

Turnover or Total Sales

Overall, it is important to keep sales increasing rather than decreasing, as the more of any item you sell, the more profit you will attract. As some elements of the sales mix, however, attract more profit than others (in this example rooms, food and beverage in that order) then the more rooms you sell, the more profit you will attract. It stands to reason that your business will be more profitable in terms of money in the bank, even if your overall turnover remained the same, but was made up of an increase in room sales of £10 000 and a decrease in food sales of £10 000, because rooms attract more profit.

For this very reason, we can see from the example shown that, because the total sales for the 3 departments is made up of a different amount, each of rooms, food and beverage between the 2 years being compared, even with a decrease in total sales (down £25 000) and a corresponding decrease in Gross Profit (down £12 800), the overall Gross Profit Margin is up by 0.57%, all explained by the shift in the sales mix.

So, we can conclude that a change in the sales mix can have a significant impact on our Gross Profit and on Gross Profit Margin, therefore it is vitally important to analyse departmental sales mix and Gross Profit to identify and act according to trends.

The average spend

Any operator needs to know how much the average customer is spending, broken down into food, wine and accommodation.

The average spend for accommodation is usually known as the average room rate.

The formula is simple:

Total Sales ÷ Total Number of Customers

or, in the case of accommodation

Total Room Sales ÷ total number of rooms occupied during the period.

This is best done daily, weekly or monthly, in order to allow the operator to spot trends and react accordingly.

Let's take total sales for one week in a restaurant of £4685, and divide by the total number of covers served, 365. The average spend is, therefore:

$$\frac{4685}{365} = £12.84 \text{ per person}$$

In another example, let's take total room sales for the month of November of £38 700.

If we divide this by the total number of rooms occupied during the month of November, of 624, then the average room rate for the month is:

$$\frac{£38\,700}{624} = £62.02$$

Whether you consider the calculated average spends to be good, bad or indifferent will depend upon how you interpret this information.

One of the best performance indicators is to compare the figures just calculated with the same period last year, or compare them with the previous period (day, week or month).

By increasing your prices, you will naturally increase your average spend, but as any marketing scholar will tell you, this action may alienate some of your customers and thus reduce your overall sales.

In this example food, wine and bar sales are analysed separately:

Daily Sales: £1554   **Number of Covers** = 60

Food Sales	1128
Wine	312
Bar	114
	1554

The average spend is therefore calculated as:

$$\frac{1554}{60} = £25.90$$

which is made up as follows:

Average Food Spend $\dfrac{1128}{60}$ =   18.80

Average Wine Spend $\dfrac{312}{60}$ =   5.20

Average Bar Spend $\dfrac{114}{60}$ =   1.90

£25.90

Remember too, that what you offer for sale and how you sell it will have an effect on average customer spend.

If you offer a three-course table d'hôte meal for £17.25, then the average spend for food will be £17.25, because that is all that is on offer. If you offer the three-course menu for £17.25 and a two-course menu for £14.75, then your average spend will be somewhere between the two possible spends.

If, out of 50 diners one evening, 25 took the two-course option and 25 took the three-course option, then the calculation of the average spend would be as follows:

25 × three-course meals @ £17.25 = **£431.25**

25 × two-course meals @ £14.75 = **£368.75**

Total Sales   = £800.00

$$\text{Average Spend} = \frac{\text{Total Sales}}{\text{No. of Customers}} = \frac{800}{50} = \underline{\textbf{£16.00}}$$

If, on the other hand, you offer an à la carte menu or an all-day menu which includes snacks, you must be aware of the possibility of a customer buying a snack and therefore spending less than, say, another customer who would like to spend more, but can't get a table to sit at.

For this very reason, some catering establishments offer snacks only at certain times of the day, or operate a minimum charge at certain times of the day (for example, peak meal times) to discourage customers who just want a coffee and thus contribute to the lowering of the average spend.

STUDENT EXERCISE

1 Explain the difference between a margin and a mark-up.
2 What is the formula for calculating Net Profit %?
3 Give 3 reasons why it is important to constantly monitor your sales mix.

4 Prepare a departmental sales mix from the following information:

	SALES		
Month	Accommodation	Food	Beverage
April	£26 000	£19 000	£10 000
May	£21 000	£17 000	£9 000
June	£23 000	£15 000	£5 000
July	£17 000	£13 500	£4 500
August	£16 000	£14 000	£6 000

5 A restaurant has a daily sales total of £2985 from 206 customers. The sales are broken down into food (£2090) and beverages (£895).
What is the average spend, per customer, and what is the average spend, per customer, on food and beverage?

6
Value Added
Tax Made
Easy

What is Value Added Tax?

Value Added Tax was first introduced in 1973. It gets its name because the tax is charged as a percentage of the value added to a product by each and every producer/supplier/or trader who handles it.

As far as the hospitality business is concerned it is, in effect, a tax which is collected by the operator from the customer, to be forwarded to the VAT department of Her Majesty's Customs and Excise Office.

Every business operator or trader whose business turns over more than around £50 000 must, by law, register with the Customs and Excise. This amount is annually revised by the Chancellor of the Exchequer for the budget.

If your business is supplied by any supplier whose invoice to you does not carry a VAT registration number, and whose invoice does not include a percentage of VAT added to the bill, then that supplier is not registered for VAT.

He or she is not registered for VAT because their business turnover is less than the current limit or threshold for registration, or because the business is exempt from VAT which means that no tax is charged by them and so no tax is payable by you!

There are three rates of VAT – a standard rate, a reduced rate on domestic fuel and power, and a zero rate.

How does VAT work?

As a hotelier, your VAT registered suppliers will charge you VAT on the goods and services they supply to you. In turn, you will mark-up the goods in order to cover all your costs and make a profit, and charge your customers a price to which you have added VAT at the standard rate.

Let's look at the simple transaction of buying a case of Cotes du Ventoux wine from your supplier and selling it on to your customer.

Your supplier's bill/invoice is £75.01 and is shown in Figure 6.1.

Invoice to:				Delivery to: (if different)		
Shellford Arms				Currie & Logan Wines Ltd		
Dockers Cross				Wine Merchants		
Shellford				Dockfield Road		
London E81 5AZ				Shellford		
				London E97 4WD		

VAT Reg. No. 123 4567 89   **Tel:** 0181 123 4567

Invoice No: 2468   **Invoice Date** 3 Aug.   **Customer Ref:** sh014

Quality	Description	VAT Rate %	Price £	VAT	Total
1 × 12	Côtes du Ventoux 1994	17.5%	63.84	11.17	75.01
		Totals:	**63.84**	**11.17**	**75.01**

Please notify us of any shortages or damages within 14 days of delivery   Please return the pink copy with your remittance

Terms are 28 days from date of invoice unless otherwise stated above

Figure 6.1 *A Sales Invoice*

This means that each bottle has cost you (75.01 ÷ 12) = £6.25, that is,

£5.32 + 93p VAT (which can be calculated by taking
(63.84 ÷ 12) = 5.32 + (11.17 ÷ 12) = 93p)

5.32 + 93p = 6.25

The Côtes du Ventoux appears on your wine list as follows:

---

8. Côtes du Ventoux 1994   £13.90

Relatively full Southern
Rhone red featuring peppery
Mediterranean fruit.
Great value!

So, how much VAT do you at the Shellford Arms actually pay to
HMCE for each bottle of Côtes du Ventoux sold?

Answer: £1.14

Here's how we arrived at that.

Assuming you decide to make 55% Gross Profit on your wines, your
selling price would be calculated as follows:

Liquor cost × 100 ÷ liquor cost % (that is, 45%).

Therefore the wine was purchased at £5.32 per bottle (excluding the
VAT of 93p, which you can claim back in your VAT return) so the
selling price is calculated as follows:

£5.32 × 100 ÷ 45 = £11.82

To this selling price we must add VAT, so:

11.82 × 17.5% = 2.07; 2.07 + 11.82 = £13.88

(A selling price of £13.88 would normally be rounded up/or down to
the nearest 5p so the price on the wine list is £13.90.)

So, we paid 93p VAT to Currie & Logan Wines Limited on each bottle
of wine, but after adding Value (that is, our mark-up) we were ready to

sell it to our customers for £11.82, but we had to add VAT onto that price of £2.07.

So we must pay HMCE £2.07 for each bottle of wine. This is called **Output Tax** but we can claim back 93p **Input Tax** so we pay the difference to them, which is:

£2.07 − 93p = £1.14 (output) − (input) = VAT payable to HMCE.

So, how much VAT do you at the Shellford Arms actually pay to HMCE for each bottle of Côtes du Ventoux sold, if you buy your Côtes du Ventoux wine from a supplier who is just starting out in business and is not yet registered for VAT? They are charging you the same net price, but do not need to charge VAT on top.

Answer: £2.07

This is calculated as follows:

£5.32 × 100 ÷ 45 = 11.82

To this price we must add VAT so

11.82 × 17.5% = 2.07; 2.07 + 11.82 = 13.88

So, we pay no VAT (Input Tax) to our wine supplier, that is, 93p less per bottle than we paid to Currie & Logan, but we pay £2.07 (Output Tax) to HMCE.

So, we have actually paid out the same amount of money from our bank account in both examples, it just flows out to different people.

Currie & Logan example:
    93p   paid to Currie & Logan
    £1.14p   paid to HMCE
    £2.07p   paid out in total

Non-VAT registered wine supplier example:
    00p   paid to non-VAT registered supplier
    £2.07p   paid to HMCE
    £2.07p   paid out in total

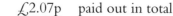

VAT fractions

Normally VAT is calculated at the appropriate percentage of a price which has first been decided without VAT (that is, a bottle of Côtes du Ventoux @ £11.82) and the tax invoice will show these separate amounts.

Sometimes, however, VAT has to be calculated or extracted from a price in which it is already included. To do this, we need the VAT fraction.

For example, if you sell a bottle of Côtes du Ventoux at £13.88 and the VAT rate is 17.5%, the amount of VAT is £2.07. But £2.07 is not 17.5% of £13.88, it is 7/47 of 13.88.

This is worked out as follows:

Rate of Tax
100 + Rate of Tax

So, with VAT at 17.5%, the VAT fraction is $\dfrac{17.5}{117.5} = \dfrac{7}{47}$

Let's explain this VAT fraction further:

$\dfrac{17.5}{117.5}$ means 17.5 divided by 117.5

17.5 is the same as $\dfrac{35}{2}$ because 35 divided by 2 = 17.5

and 117.5 is the same as $\dfrac{235}{2}$

because 235 divided by 2 = 117.5

So far so good!

So $\dfrac{35}{2} \div \dfrac{235}{2}$ is the same as $\dfrac{35}{2} \times \dfrac{2}{235}$

If we cancel the 2s and take the other numbers to their lowest common denominator by dividing by 5, we get:

$$\frac{35 \div 5}{235 \div 5} = \frac{7}{47}$$

Every VAT rate will have its own VAT fraction. Suppose the Chancellor of the Exchequer were to announce a higher rate of VAT at the next budget of say 18%, this would mean adding 18 per cent to the intended selling price for Output Tax.

The new VAT fraction would be $\dfrac{18}{118}$ of the final price.

The new calculation would be as follows:

$$\frac{18}{118} = \frac{36}{2} \div \frac{236}{2} = \frac{36}{2} \times \frac{2}{236}$$

By cancelling the 2s and dividing the other numbers by 4 we have:

$$\frac{36}{2} \times \frac{2}{236} = \frac{9}{1} \times \frac{1}{59} = \frac{9}{59}$$

This is our new VAT fraction which we apply to any calculation where we are calculating what part of our VAT inclusive daily takings is VAT Output Tax and must therefore be paid over to HMCE (once we have deducted our Input Tax).

Let's use both these calculations on a bottle of Côtes du Ventoux from Currie & Logan.

The bottle has cost us £5.32p. We have added value because of the interior decor of the restaurant, the ambience, the highly trained kitchen brigade and the highly trained and personable waiting staff.

We have calculated that we can sell this wine at £11.82 to which we must add VAT.

Cost	VAT @ 17.5%	Selling Price
11.82	2.07	13.88
Cost	VAT @ 18%	Selling Price
11.82	2.13	13.95

By using the appropriate VAT fractions we can work back to £2.07 and £2.13 respectively in working out the VAT content of a bottle of wine being sold at £13.88 (VAT @ 17.5%) and a bottle of wine being sold at £13.95 (VAT @ 18%).

Calculations are as follows:

17.5% Rate $13.88 \times \dfrac{7}{47} = 2.07$

18% Rate $13.95 \times \dfrac{9}{59} = 2.13$

The VAT Return

Every 3 months (quarterly) the VAT computer sends out an official form called a VAT Return.

Having noted your sales and purchases for the 3 months, the VAT paid to you as part of your sales (Output Tax) is calculated as is the VAT you have paid out, which has been added to your purchases (Input Tax).

By deducting your Input Tax from your Output Tax you will thus calculate the amount owed to HMCE.

There are currently 9 boxes to fill in on a VAT Return.

VAT due in this period on **Sales** and other outputs	1. ☐
VAT due in this period on **acquisitions** from other **EC Member States**	2. ☐
Total VAT due (**the sum of boxes 1 and 2**)	3. ☐
VAT reclaimed in this period on **purchases** and other inputs (including acquisitions from the EC)	4. ☐
Net VAT to be paid to HMCE or reclaimed by you (Difference between boxes 3 and 4)	5. ☐

Total value of **Sales** and all other outputs excluding any VAT. **Include your box 8 figure**   6. ☐

Total value of **purchases** and all other inputs excluding any VAT. **Include your box 9 figure**   7. ☐

Total value of all **suppliers** of goods and related services, excluding any VAT, to other **EC Member States**   8. ☐

Total value of all **acquisitions** goods and related services, excluding any VAT, from other **EC Member States**   9. ☐

Notes

Box 1
Show the VAT due on all goods and services you supplied in this period.

Box 2
Show the VAT due (but not paid) on all goods and related services you acquired in this period from other EC Member States.

Box 3
Show the total amount of VAT due, that is the sum of boxes 1 and 2. This is your total **Output** tax.

Box 4
Show the amount of VAT deductible on any business purchases including acquisitions of goods and related services from other EC Member States. This is your **Input** tax.

Box 5
If this amount is under £1, you need not send any payment, nor will any repayment be made to you, but you must still fill in this form and send it to the VAT Central Unit.

Boxes 6 and 7
In box 6 show the value excluding VAT of your total outputs (supplies of goods and services). Include zero rated, exempt outputs and EC supplies from box 8.

In box 7 show the value excluding VAT of all your inputs (purchases of goods and services). Include zero rated, exempt inputs and EC acquisitions from box 9.

Boxes 8 and 9
EC Trade Only
Use these boxes if you have supplied goods to or acquired goods from another EC Member State. Include related services such as transport costs, where these form part of the invoice or contract price. The figures should exclude VAT.

Currently the other EC Member States are:
Austria, Belgium, Denmark, Finland, France, Germany, Greece, Ireland, Italy, Luxembourg, Netherlands, Portugal, Spain and Sweden.

VAT Inspections

Usually during your first year of registration, and at future dates, you will receive a VAT inspection visit.

If you have made a genuine error, or have claimed input tax wrongly, the inspector will make an assessment and issue a demand for payment. Alternatively there may be some financial penalty, but this is likely to be fairly nominal in the case of a genuine error or lack of initial understanding.

Annual Accounting Scheme for small businesses

The VAT Office have now introduced an Annual Accounting Scheme for any business which has been registered for 12 months or more and whose taxable turnover (net of VAT) is below £300 000.

This benefits the smaller business because:
- there is only one return required, therefore there is less risk of penalties;
- there are fewer deadlines;
- there is an easing of cash flow;
- there is reduction of some paperwork;
- you get an extra month to complete;
- there are fixed interim payments, which may be quarterly × 3 or monthly × 9 depending upon your turnover.

The interim payments are based upon your previous year's VAT returns and will be 20% of your year's net liability if the payments are quarterly, and 10% of your previous year's net liability if your payments are monthly.

Cash Accounting Scheme

This scheme is available to those who are VAT registered and whose turnover is less than £350 000. It is helpful to businesses where customers are given extended periods of credit and where bad debts may be a problem. The scheme allows you to account for VAT on the basis of payments you receive and make, rather than on tax invoices you issue and receive.

Service charge

From time to time there is great debate within the hospitality industry as to the rights and wrongs of levying a service charge on customers' bills in some hotels and restaurants.

One school of thought is that customers should not be 'expected' to pay for a service involuntarily, whilst the other school of thought believes in the service charge levy being given either directly to staff or being used to supplement wages. Whatever your view, should a service charge be levied, it is simple to calculate.

A service charge may be levied from 10% to 20%, but much over 15% nowadays is regarded as expensive – 10% or 12.5% is most common.

To add the service charge, use the % button on your calculator.

Examples

Add 10% service charge to a bill of £58.40.

Formula £58.40 × 10% + = £64.24

10% of 58.40 is 5.84

Therefore, £58.40 + £5.84 = £64.24

If 12.5% service charge was to be added to the same bill, the answer would be as follows:

£58.40 × 12.5% + = £65.70

£58.40 + £7.30 = £65.70

So, let's remind ourselves of how we calculate our selling price by applying a pre-determined Gross Profit Margin (GP%). Then after we have calculated that, calculate the selling price, including VAT. Figure 6.2 on page 70 contains the questions for calculating selling price, and Figure 6.3 on page 71 contains the answers.

Example

Food Cost 54p

Require GP% 49%

Because the GP% and the FC% **must** add up to 100% the FC% must be 100% − 49% = 51%

So, to set the selling price

$$SP = \frac{FC}{FC\%} \times 100 \quad \text{i.e.,} \quad \frac{0.54p}{51} \times 100 = £1.05$$

To add VAT @ 17.5% the formula is:

£1.05 × 1.175 = £1.23

Now do the rest.

SETTING SELLING PRICES

Food cost	Gross Profit %	Food cost %	Selling price	Selling price inc VAT
1. 54p	49%			
2. 18p	56%			
3. 32p	58%			
4. 21p	60%			
5. 86p	50%			
6. 41p	50%			
7. 23.5p	55%			
8. 85p	49%			
9. 76p	34%			
10. 65p	60%			
11. 95p	65%			
12. £1.22	55%			

Figure 6.2 *Setting selling prices*

SETTING SELLING PRICES

Food cost	Gross Profit %	Food cost %	Selling price	Selling price inc VAT
1. 54p	49%	51%	1.05	1.23
2. 18p	56%	44%	0.41	0.48
3. 32p	58%	42%	0.76	0.89
4. 21p	60%	40%	0.52	0.61
5. 86p	50%	50%	1.72	2.02
6. 41p	50%	50%	0.82	0.96
7. 23.5p	55%	45%	0.52	0.61
8. 85p	49%	51%	1.66	1.95
9. 76p	34%	66%	1.15	1.35
10. 65p	60%	40%	1.62	1.90
11. 95p	65%	35%	2.71	3.18
12. £1.22	55%	45%	2.71	3.18

Figure 6.3 *Setting selling prices*

STUDENT EXERCISE

1 You have been asked to price the following new dishes for your menu, inclusive of VAT, and a Gross Profit Margin of 67%. You have calculated the food costs as follows:

a Crab and Ginger Mousse £0.85p
b Fresh Tuna Steak with onion marmalade £2.63p
c Saute of beef fillet with a pepper sauce £1.72p
d Escalope of Turkey, Cordon Bleu £0.71p
e Fruit filled filo baskets £0.80p
f Profiteroles with Martian Sauce £0.58p

2 According to the Campaign for Real Ale, the average price of a pint of real ale bought in a pub is now £1.64p (*Caterer and Hotel Keeper*, 31 July–6 August 1997). How much is that exclusive of VAT?

3 Under normal circumstances and excluding any special arrangements, how often must a VAT return be made to HMCE?

4 Define Output tax and Input tax as they apply to VAT.

7
The Basics of Food Costing

Let's put apple pie and cream or apple pie and ice cream onto our menu.

Let's assume that the apple pie will sell at £2.25p per portion, inclusive of VAT. As the VAT goes to the Customs and Excise, we have to de-VAT the £2.25p so that we are left with the net selling price (exclusive of VAT).

By taking £2.25p and putting that into our calculator and dividing it by 1.175, we get a net selling price of £1.91489 (call it £1.92p). This is the same as using the VAT fraction:

$$£2.25 \times \frac{7}{47} = 33p$$

£2.25p − 33p = £1.92p

Let's assume that we wish for a 65% Gross Profit. We now need to work out what the cost of producing the portion will be in order that we can achieve the Gross Profit of 65%. So if the Gross Profit is 65%, then the food cost represents 35%, because they must both add up to 100%.

Food cost percentage

We know, therefore, that the food cost percentage we want is 35%, therefore £1.91p × 35% = 67p. This can be checked by taking £1.91p and multiplying it by the Gross Profit percentage which is 65%, so £1.91p × 65% = £1.24p. £1.24p + 67p therefore equals the selling price of £1.91p, so we have there

65% + 35% = 100% or £1.24p + 67p = £1.91p.

We now know that the cost of the apple pie must be no more than 67p per portion. So how many portions are we going to get out of the apple pie, or in other words, what is the portion yield?

For the sake of these calculations, let's make sure that we will get 8 portions out of the apple pie.

The cost is 67p and the selling price is £1.91p, excluding VAT. This represents a Gross Profit of 65%. Eight portions of apple pie therefore cost 8 × 67p = £5.36p and 8 × £1.91p represents the selling price of the whole pie, exclusive of VAT (that is, £15.28p). The difference between these two figures is £15.28p − £5.36p = £9.92p, which is the Gross Profit and the Gross Profit of £9.92 represents a Gross Profit percentage of 65%. This can be checked by taking £15.28p and multiplying it by 65%:

$$£15.28p \times 65\% = £9.93p$$

(note there is a differential in pence which will happen from time to time depending on what calculator you are using).

But what would happen if the total cost of the ingredients of the pie was more than £5.36p, or if instead of getting eight portions at £1.91p, which represents total sales of £15.28p, we only got 7 portions at £1.91p, which represents total sales of £13.37p? The question is, what would this do to the Gross Profit?

First let's look at the cost of the pie.

Regardless of who is making the pie, it needs to be made to a standard recipe, otherwise it may be too expensive, which means the Gross Profit will not be achieved. In other words, in this example, the food cost will be greater than 35%, that is greater than £5.36p. If the cost is less, it may compromise the quality and customers may feel that they are unwilling to spend £2.25p (£1.91p exclusive of VAT) on purchasing a piece of apple pie. This, therefore, necessitates that we have standard recipes which yield a standard number of portions.

Once a standard recipe has been decided, and this may be done by a tasting panel which may well be a brigade of chefs, many decisions have to be made regarding portion size. Is it to be a tray pie? A round pie? Are the portions to be square? Are the portions to be slices? How will the presentation take place? How much ice cream goes with it? How much cream goes with it? What happens if the customer asks for ice cream *and* pouring cream?

So, regardless of how many chefs operate in any kitchen, regardless of what type of catering operation the kitchen represents, it is vital that standard recipes are used. This will allow for dish costing to take place, which means that the Gross Profit, which is also known as the kitchen percentage, remains as required.

Dish costing

For a lot of caterers and hospitality businesses, dish costing appears to be a tedious process. However, a relatively short time spent in costing out all menu items will result in consistent high quality goods being produced at a selling price which will attract the required Gross Profit. First of all you require your standard recipe which will normally be for a specified number of portions.

Using a recipe/dish costing record will allow you to keep a note of the content of dishes, and will help you to keep a record of garnishes and accompaniments. It will also help you with pricing decisions and with any amendments that are required for the recipe.

An example of a dish costing form is included in Figure 7.1 on page 76 and requires you to put down on paper the name of the dish and the number of portions yielded from that particular recipe; the quantity of each ingredient; the cost in the unit of which the ingredients are bought (that is pounds, kilos, litres, pints and so on) and the proportionate cost.

Care should be taken when compiling a dish costing form to ensure that units are either imperial or metric and not mixed, that is pounds and kilos or litre and pints.

At the end of the dish costing form you should have a total cost for the total number of portions, and therefore the total cost divided by the number of portions becomes the portion cost.

Name of Dish			
Number of Portions			
Quantity	**Ingredients**	**Unit Cost**	**Cost**
TOTAL COST (Above) =			
PORTION COST = **No. of Portions**			

Figure 7.1 *Dish Costing Form*

The cost of ingredients in any dish costing should be monitored regularly and should be done at least four times per year. As prices increase, it will be necessary to pass these price increases on to the end user (the customer) in order to maintain the required Gross Profit. If this is not done, then profits will suffer.

Let's now take a standard recipe and transfer it to a dish costing form, but just before we do so, let's take some time to remind ourselves of calculating the price of ounces (oz) if we know the price of a pound (lb), the price of grammes (g) if we know the price of a kilogramme (kg), and the price of parts of pints and litres.

There are 16 ounces in one pound.

So, if we know the price of a pound of sultanas, we can find the price of 10 ounces by simply dividing the amount, per pound, by 16 (to give us the cost per ounce), then multiply by 10 which will give us the cost per 10 ounces.

1lb Sultanas cost 98p
There are 16ozs in a pound so
16oz Sultanas cost 98p

1oz Sultanas cost $\dfrac{98p}{16} = 0.06p$

10ozs Sultanas cost $\dfrac{98}{16} \times 10 = £0.60p$

If we know the price of a kilogramme (kilo) of sultanas, we can find the cost of 280 grammes of sultanas by simply dividing the amount per kilo by 1000 (because there are 1000 grammes in a kilogramme) then multiply by 280 which will give us the cost per 280 grammes.

1kg of sultanas cost £2.16p
There are 1000g in a kg so
1000g of sultanas cost £2.16p

1 gramme of sultanas cost $\dfrac{2.16}{1000} = 0.00216$

280 grammes cost $\dfrac{2.16}{1000} \times 280 = £0.60p$

There is a simpler way to calculate metric weights.

$$280 \text{ grammes} = 280\text{ths of } 1000 \text{ or } \frac{280}{1000}$$

280 grammes is, in fact, 0.280 of 1 kilogramme, so, $2.16 \times 0.280 = £0.60$

Similarly, if you know the cost of one pint of stock or soup, then the price of 6 fluid ounces will be as follows:

One pint = 20 fluid ounces

1 pint of beef stock costs   23p
20 fluid ounces of beef stock costs   23p

1 fluid ounce of beef stock costs $\dfrac{0.23}{20} = 0.0115$

6 fluid ounces cost $\dfrac{0.23}{20} \times 6 = 0.069$ (call it 7p)

In addition, if you know the cost of 1 litre of beef stock, then the cost of 1.9 litres will be the cost of 1 litre $\times$ 1.9.

For example

Beef stock costs 40p per litre, so 1.9 litres cost $0.40 \times 1.9 = £0.76\text{p}$

Let's look at the following recipe for 10 portions of Beef Olives

> 1.45 kilos lean top rump
> 145 grammes stuffing
> 130 grammes dripping
> 375 grammes carrots
> 375 grammes Spanish onions
> 85 grammes plain flour
> 55 grammes tomato purée
> 1.9 litres brown stock
> 1 × bouquet garni

Your latest supplier list gives you the costs as follows:

Beef	£5.95 per kilo
Stuffing	£3.40 per kilo
Dripping	£1.50 per kilo
Carrots	£0.30 per kilo
Spanish Onions	£0.54 per kilo
Plain flour	£0.45 per kilo
Tomato Purée	£0.87 per kilo
Brown Stock	£0.40 per litre
Bouquet Garni	£19 per pack of 100

Figure 7.2 on page 80 shows the calculations on the standard dish costing form, but let's work this through item by item.

■ **1.450kg of Lean Top Rump Beef @ £5.95 per kg.**

$$\frac{£5.95}{1000} \times 1450 = £8.6275 \text{ (call it £8.63)}$$

or

£5.95 × 1.450 = £8.6275 (call it £8.63)

■ **145g Stuffing @ £3.40 per kg**

$$\frac{£3.40}{1000} \times 145 = £0.493 \text{ (call it 49p)}$$

or

£3.40 × 0.145 = £0.493 (call it 49p)

■ **130g Dripping @ £1.50 per kg**

$$\frac{£1.50}{1000} \times 130 = £0.195 \text{ (call it 19p)}$$

or

£1.50 × 0.130 = £0.195 (call it 19p)

■ **375g Carrots @ £0.30p per kg**

$$\frac{£0.30}{1000} \times 375 = £0.1125 \text{ (call it 11p)}$$

or

£0.30 × 0.375 = £0.1125 (call it 11p)

■ **375g Spanish Onions @ £0.54p per kg**

$$\frac{£0.54}{1000} \times 375 = £0.2025 \text{ (call it 20p)}$$

or

£0.54 × 0.375 = £0.2025 (call it 20p)

■ **85g Plain Flour @ £0.45p per kg**

$$\frac{£0.45}{1000} \times 85 = £0.03825 \text{ (call it 4p)}$$

or

£0.45 × 0.085 = £0.03825 (call it 4p)

■ **55g Tomato Purée @ £0.87p per kg**

$$\frac{£0.87}{1000} \times 55 = £0.04785 \text{ (call it 5p)}$$

or

£0.87 × 0.055 = £0.04785 (call it 5p)

■ **1.9 Litres Brown Stock @ £0.40p per Litre**

$$\frac{£0.40}{1000} \times 1900 = £0.76p$$

or

£0.40 × 1.9 = £0.76p

■ **1 × Bouquet Garni @ 19p each**

1 × 19p = 19p

Name of Dish:	Beef Olives

Number of Portions:	10

Quantity	Ingredients	Unit Cost	Cost	
			£	**pence**
1.450kg	Lean Top Rump Beef	5.95kg	8	63
145g	Stuffing	3.40kg	0	49
130g	Dripping	1.50kg	0	19
375g	Carrots	0.30kg	0	11
375g	Spanish Onions	0.54kg	0	20
85g	Plain Flour	0.45kg	0	04
55g	Tomato Puree	0.87kg	0	05
1.9 litres	Brown Stock	0.40 litres	0	76
1	Bouquet Garni	19p	0	19
		Total	**10**	**66**

$$\text{Portion Cost} = \frac{\text{TOTAL COST (Above)}}{\text{No. of Portions}} = \frac{10.66}{10} \quad \boxed{£1.07p}$$

Figure 7.2 *Dish Costing Form*

The total cost of the dish is £10.66, so the cost of one portion is £10.66 divided by 10
= 1.066 (call it £1.07)

What we will now do is calculate the selling price, inclusive of VAT, if the required Gross Profit is to be 65%.

Remember the formula:

$$SP = \frac{\text{Food Cost}}{\text{FC}\%} \times 100$$

$$SP = \frac{£1.07}{35} \times 100 = £3.06$$

£3.06 plus VAT @ 17.5% is:

3.06 × 1.175 = £3.5955 (call it £3.60)

Costing a breakfast

When I run training courses on food costing and setting profitable selling prices, delegates often say how difficult it is to calculate the cost of breakfast because everybody has a different combination of menu items.

The best way to tackle such a situation is to monitor closely what you sell over a period of perhaps 10 days. This will give you an average cost per breakfast, and allow you to price accordingly or make the necessary food cost allowances for your Bed and Breakfast rate. For example, if Bed and Breakfast is selling at £57.50p, inclusive, how much are you allowing the chef out of that £57.50p for a breakfast food cost?

In many establishments today breakfast is served from a buffet, where hot breakfast items are either plated and brought from the kitchen or presented in hot containers/hot plates for guests to serve themselves. Whichever system is in use, you need to list all possible breakfast menu items which may be required, and monitor them (see Figure 7.3).

Breakfast costing

■ For the menu items estimate the number of portions of each item that you have served over a given period.

■ Using the latest prices, calculate the total cost of serving, say, 20 breakfasts.

■ Add on wastage allowance of 5% and calculate the cost of the average breakfast.

Menu Offered	Portions Served per 20 Breakfasts	Portion Cost (pence)	Total Cost
Fruit Juice	18	12	2.16
Fruit Compote	4	23	0.92
Fresh Grapefruit Segments	4	22	0.88
Cereal and Milk	10	19	1.90
Porridge and Milk	2	17	0.34
Yoghurt	5	18	0.90
Bacon (2) and Egg (1)	6	71	4.26
Sausage (2) and Egg (1)	2	38	0.76
Bacon (2) Sausage (1) Egg (1) & Tomato ($\frac{1}{2}$)	8	85	6.80
Scrambled Eggs (2) on Toast	2	22	0.44
Boiled Eggs (2)	2	14	0.28
Toast (2 slices)	20	8	1.60
Butter (2 portions)	20	6	1.20
Marmalade/Jam (1 portion)	18	15	2.70
Tea (2 cups)	12	3	0.36
Coffee (2 cups)	8	6	0.48

25.98

+ **Wastage Allowance 5%**   **1.30**

27.28

Average Cost Per Breakfast $\dfrac{27.28}{20} =$ **£1.36**

Figure 7.3 *How to cost a breakfast*

Question

If the selling price of your table d'hôte dinner is £16.95p, inclusive of VAT, and you require a Gross Profit (kitchen) percentage of 62%, how much do you have to spend on food cost per person?

Let's do this calculation step by step:

1 Calculate Selling Price, excluding VAT
2 Calculate Food Cost %
3 Calculate Food Cost

1 Calculate Selling Price, excluding VAT
  Selling Price, including VAT = £16.95p
  To de-VAT an amount, you either use the VAT fraction or divide by 1.175

$$16.95 \times \frac{7}{47} = 2.52$$

  $16.95 - 2.52 = £14.43$
  Alternatively:
  $16.95 \div 1.175 = £14.4255$ (call it £14.43)
  The Selling Price, exclusive of VAT is, therefore, £14.43.

2 Calculate the Food Cost %
  If the Gross Profit percentage required is 62%, the Food Cost percentage must be
  100% less 62% = 38%

3 Calculate the Food Cost %
  So 38% of £14.43 is $14.43 \times 38\% = 5.48$
  This can be checked by calculating the Gross Profit from the Gross Profit percentage
  62% of 14.43 is $14.43 \times 62\% = 8.95$
  This can be double-checked by adding
  $38\% + 62\% = 100\%$
  $5.48 + 8.95 = £14.43$

So, provided you can produce a balanced menu and a menu that your customers will want to eat from, you must produce your two-course table d'hôte meal for a food cost of no more than £5.48, otherwise you will not achieve your kitchen percentage (GP%) of 62%.

To convert grammes to ounces, we divide by 28.3495. So to find the cost of 1oz, when we know the cost of 250 grams, the following calculation is done:

250 grams divided by 28.3495 = 8.8184976, so the cost of 1oz is 87p divided by 8.8184976 = £0.0986562 = 9.9p or 10p to the nearest two significant figures.

A Ready Reckoner is provided in the Glossary at the back of this book.

STUDENT EXERCISE

Cost the following three menus and price them as follows using the dish costing forms on pages 76 and 80.

1 Pork with mushrooms, chillies and tomatoes, to have a GP margin of 68% and the addition of VAT.

2 Smoked chicken salad with mango and grapefruit to represent a food cost of 34% and the addition of VAT.

3 Fried fillet of cod with caper sauce to represent a food cost of 38% and the addition of VAT.

Name of Dish: Pork with Mushrooms Chillies and Tomatoes		No. of Portions: 10	
Quantity	Ingredients	Unit Cost	Cost
10	Pork loin steaks (180g each)	£3.25 per kilo	
75ml	Olive Oil	£2.60 per litre	
200ml	Sherry	£3.60 per litre	
300g	Tomatoes	£1.40 per kilo	
20g	Granulated Sugar	£1.00 per kilo	
150g	Red Chillies	£8.00 per kilo	
150g	Green Chillies	£4.00 per kilo	
300g	Oyster Mushrooms	£7.20 per kilo	
5	Red Peppers	25p each	
1 bunch	Spring Onions	35p bunch	
6	Bay Leaves	1p each	
	Fresh Rosemary	10p	
	Flat Leaf Pastry	15p	

PORTION COST = $\dfrac{\text{Total Cost (above)}}{\text{No. of Portions}}$ =

Name of Dish: Smoked Chicken Salad
With Mango & Grapefruit   No. of Portions: 10

Quantity	Ingredients	Unit Cost	Cost
4	Smoked Chicken Breast	£1.50 each	
4	Grapefruit	35p each	
4	Mangoes	£7 per box of 12	
1	Oak Leaf Lettuce	£6 per box of 12	
1	Curly Endive	£10 per box of 12	
1	Lollo Rosso	£7 per box of 12	
85g	Ground Ginger	£3.75 per kilo	
250ml	Mayonnaise	£1.96 per litre	
1 bunch	Thyme	£1.20 per bunch	

$$\text{PORTION COST} = \frac{\text{Total Cost (above)}}{\text{No. of Portions}} =$$

Name of Dish: Fried Fillet of Cod
With Caper Sauce   No. of Portions: 12

Quantity	Ingredients	Unit Cost	Cost
2 × kg	Cod fillet (approx 170g per person)	£4.20 per kg	
100ml	Olive Oil (for frying)	£2.60 per litre	
1	Finely chopped Spanish Onion	20p	
100gm	Butter	£3.50 per kilo	
100ml	White Wine	£3.50 per litre	
150g	Spinach	£5.50 for 4.5kg	
150g	Capers	£5 per kg	
	Salt	1p	
	Pepper	1p	

$$\text{PORTION COST} = \frac{\text{Total Cost (above)}}{\text{No. of Portions}} =$$

8
The Basics
of Beverage
Costing

If you are in the pub business or if you hold a licence to sell alcohol in your café, restaurant, hotel or guest house, then it makes sense to sell your drinks profitably.

As with selling food, there is an industry norm and you will need to achieve a certain Gross Profit from selling your drinks, otherwise you will not be achieving enough profit to pay the rest of your bills.

Most drinks which you buy are bought by a specific unit of measure, for example 1 pint, $\frac{1}{2}$ pint, or a measured glass. Once you find the cost of each of these, then you apply a formula and sell it for a profit which is acceptable to you and the customer. This applies to alcoholic and non-alcoholic beverages, the alcoholic beverages being beers, wines, spirits and liqueurs and the non-alcoholic beverages being soft drinks, mixers, teas and coffees.

Let us first look at the costing and pricing we require to use for alcoholic beverages. The first thing that we will look at is a pint of beer.

Beer can be purchased in kegs containing anything from 72 to 288 pints. Barrels containing lesser amounts from the smaller, more specialised breweries are also produced in addition, of course, to bottled and canned beers.

If a barrel of beer costs £60 and yields 88 pints, then £60 being the cost divided by 88 being the number of pints = the cost of a pint = 68p.

The industry norm for the Gross Profit percentage to be expected from a pint of draught beer varies considerably depending upon the type of licensed outlet.

■ In hotels and restaurants the liquor Gross Profit will be between 45% and 65%.

■ In the banqueting department it is seldom below 55% and can go up to 70%.

■ In pubs liquor Gross Profit is usually 40% to 55%.

■ In private clubs Gross Profit is as low as 25% to 45%.

Remember that Gross Profit percentage plus liquor cost percentage must always add up to 100% (in exactly the same way as Gross Profit percentage plus food cost percentage must always add up to 100).

The format is as follows, and in this example the GP% is 45%.

Selling price = liquor cost × 100 ÷ liquor cost percentage.

In this case, the liquor cost is 68p and the liquor cost percentage is 55% because the required gross profit is 45%.

So the formula is as follows:

$$SP = \frac{\text{Liquor Cost}}{\text{Liquor Cost \%}} \times 100$$

$$SP = \frac{0.68}{55} \times 100$$

(Liquor cost % must be 55% if GP% is 45%!)

SP = 1.236 (call it 1.24)

To which we must add VAT at the standard rate

£1.24 × 17.5% + = £1.457 (call it £1.46)

For bottled beers, the industry norm should be around 50%, for wines 55%, for spirits and liqueurs approximately 65% and for soft drinks and mixers, approximately 65%.

What we therefore achieve as an average Gross Profit percentage will obviously depend on how much of each of the different types of beverages we sell.

Kegs

The most common size of kegs contain 50 litres and 100 litres which correspond to 88 and 176 pints respectively, assuming there is no wastage.

The table below shows the keg sizes and the number of gallons/pints/litres contained in each.

KEG SIZES		
Gallons	**Pints**	**Litres**
9	72	40 litres
11	88	50 litres
18	144	81 litres
22	176	100 litres
36	288	163 litres

Weights and Measures law

Your local Consumer and Trading Standards Officers ensure that licensed premises comply with the law when selling alcohol.

Draught beer and cider must be sold in quantities of $\frac{1}{3}$ pint, $\frac{1}{2}$ pint or multiples of $\frac{1}{2}$ pint, such as 1 pint.

Government stamped brim measure or line measure glasses or Government stamped meters must be used.

This does not apply to bottled and canned beers and ciders or shandies.

Spirits

The four specified spirits:

Whisky, gin, rum and vodka must, by law, be sold in metric measures of 25mls or 35mls (millilitres) or multiples thereof. The measure selected must be used throughout the premises and for all of the four spirits.

The measures used must be a stamped optic marked with the quantity dispensed or a stamped thimble measure.

Any other alcoholic beverages sold by measure must be dispensed using either a stamped optic or a stamped thimble measure.

Soft drinks

Soft drinks and shandies, if sold by a specified measure, have to be sold by metric measure. It is a good idea, therefore, to avoid specifying a measure and merely to describe them as 'large' or 'small'. Remember, you need to know the size of the large and small portions, so that you can apply your formula for calculating the selling price once you know the cost of the portion/unit!

Wine

Wine sold by the glass has to be sold in metric measures of either 125mls or 175mls or multiples thereof.

Both measures can be used in the one establishment, for example small or large glass. The wine must be served into a Government stamped glass or from a Government stamped measure.

Wine sold by the carafe may be sold in the following quantities:

250mls, 500mls, 750mls or 1000mls (1 litre)

Carafes must be stamped with the quantities.

In all these cases, the law is helping you control your portions by specifying the quantities sold.

STUDENT EXERCISE

1 If a 100 litre barrel of beer was purchased for £118.00p, how much should you sell a pint for if you require a Gross Profit % of 60%? Remember to add VAT onto the selling price.

2 How many 25ml measures of vodka are there in a litre bottle?

3 If a litre bottle of vodka costs £12.80p, excluding VAT, and a pub wants to make a Gross Profit margin of 55%, what is the selling price of a 25ml measure of vodka?

4 A 75cl bottle of 1995 New Zealand Sauvignon Blanc sells for £12.50p, including VAT. The Gross Profit margin is 55%.

What is the cost per bottle, excluding VAT?

How many large (175ml) and how many small (125ml) glasses will a 75cl bottle yield?

How much would you have to sell the large and small glasses for (including VAT) to achieve the same Gross Profit % as selling by the bottle?

9
The Basics of Room Costing

It is relatively easy, as we have discovered in previous chapters, to find the cost of a pint of beer or the cost of a dozen eggs, but how much does a room cost?

Once we know the price of beer or the price of a dozen eggs, we can apply a formula and set a selling price. This is obviously much more difficult, not to say impossible, when looking at the cost of a room or accommodation.

There are two types of costs involved in the sale of accommodation and these are divided into **fixed costs** and **variable costs**.

Variable costs include laundry and items such as give-aways or freebies like soaps, shower caps, shoe shine, stationery, book matches and so on. There are also variable elements of labour and overheads.

The principle of accommodation costing is therefore to cover fixed costs and these are items such as rent, rates, insurance and depreciation, as well as the variable costs.

Where the costing of food and beverages is concerned, the gross profit covers fixed costs and the net profit. In other words, the difference between the buying price and the selling price is the contribution that item makes to running the business with a contribution to profit as well.

This principle is also used as far as pricing accommodation is concerned. In order, therefore, to price accommodation, we must find out what fixed costs are and what profit is required and this needs to be done from an annual point of view. Once we know the annual fixed costs and the annual profit required, the amount is then spread over the whole year and divided by the number of rooms that we have.

This will therefore give us a fixed cost per room per night, but the main problem here is that such a calculation assumes that all the rooms in the hotel are full every night of the week. This is obviously not the case, and it is therefore vitally important that accurate records are kept in order to establish the occupancy levels from month to month, week to week and indeed, day to day. On this basis, budgets can be set for the year (where a new build is concerned market research is carried out locally to establish what levels of occupancy are already prevailing in the area). Let's put that into an example.

Room costing

Example

150 bedroom hotel with an average room occupancy of 73% (that is, 109 rooms occupied per night) which has fixed costs of £770 000 and has a net profit target of £350 000. The contribution each room must make is as follows:

Fixed costs + net profit ÷ number of rooms sold per year.
£770 000 + £350 000 ÷ (150 × 365 × 73%)
£1 120 000 ÷ 39 967 = £28.02p

Let's say that the variable cost (laundry + 'freebies' + variable labour and overheads) is £10.50p per room, per night.

If we add both of these together, we can fix a selling price of £28.02 + £10.50p = £38.52p (net of VAT).

With VAT, the price is £38.52p × 17.5% + = £45.26p.

To this we will have to add the selling price of meals if we wish to quote customers' bed and breakfast or dinner, bed and breakfast rates.

There are some crucial learning points from the above exercise.

1 The above contribution and the variable cost is based on a per room basis. Many hotels may wish to quote a per person rate, which means that the number of guests (or sleepers) that the hotel can accommodate is used instead of number of rooms.

2 If room occupancy levels rise above 73%, that is if sales increase, then net profit increases. Conversely, if room occupancy levels fall below 73%, that is if sales decrease, then profits fall accordingly.

Think also what happens to your profit (because you will have to pay the bills incurred from your fixed costs) if you start discounting your accommodation selling price before you have earned enough money to pay for your overheads.

If you are 'on target' to achieve your budgets (see Chapter 16 for more information), then discounting rooms by promoting special events or weekend breaks can increase your room revenue, but will not obviously contribute as much profit as selling the rooms at 'rack rate', where 'rack rate' is the rate advertised on the 'rack' by any accommodation provider (that is, the highest price charged).

Let's spend a moment or two longer studying our 150 bedroom hotel, with 73% annual room occupancy.

Of the £28.02p which represents fixed costs and net profit, the fixed costs part of the £28.02 is £19.26, and the net profit is £8.76p. This is calculated as follows:

$$\text{Fixed Costs} \frac{770\,000}{39\,967} + \text{Net Profit} \frac{350\,000}{39\,967}$$

$$= £19.26p + £8.76p = £28.02p$$

Let's assume that your budget for April (a 30 day month) at 73% occupancy means that you must achieve 30 × 109 room nights (where 109 represents 73% of the 150 rooms you have available), that is 3270 room nights.

Let's say that you have had an exceptional first 26 days for the month of April and you have already achieved your 3270 room nights at the rate of £40.56. This means that, in three weeks, you have sold enough rooms, at a high enough rate, to pay for your fixed costs for that month and your net profit for that month. So, the only thing you need to pay for when you sell rooms for the last 4 days of April, is the variable costs of £10.50p per room, per night.

As your fixed costs have already been paid, anything more than £10.50p, which you get for the room, becomes pure net profit.

You can compare this method of pricing to that of buying a seat on an aircraft. It is a well-known fact that the business community, by buying business class airline fares, and those other 'full-fare' paying passengers, pay for the overheads, plus the required profit on each flight.

Thereafter, in exactly the same way as room costing, it is only the variable expenses that airline companies will then have to cover, so airline seats will be sold through travel agents and sometimes direct to the public at a greatly reduced rate. Yet, like the hotel, the airline will still make money.

It is when accommodation operators do not do their sums first, regarding fixed costs, profit, variable costs and occupancy levels, and when they do not budget correctly, that things begin to go wrong – especially when they are selling rooms where contributions are not enough to pay the bills, let alone contribute to profit!

STUDENT EXERCISE

1 Fix a room selling price, inclusive of VAT, for a 60 bedroom hotel with an average room occupancy of 68% which has fixed costs of £310 000 and has a net profit target of £120 000.
If your breakfast food cost is £1.20p and your table d'hôte dinner cost is £6.40p, what will you sell your dinner, bed and breakfast 'package' for if you require to make a food Gross Profit % of 62%? (Don't forget to add the VAT onto the selling price.)

10
The Basics of Function/ Banqueting Costing

Many hotels or catering operations will offer conference and banqueting facilities. When we are dealing with a large number of people who will all be eating the same meal at the same time, then it is possible to be much more accurate in the calculation of the cost of such food and service. It is possible to apply the selling price formula, and in this case, the industry norm for Gross Profit is in the region of 55%–70%. What we do, therefore, is find the direct costs that are involved for the particular banquet or function, which are food and labour, and add on a percentage which will cover fixed overheads and a percentage for profit. We therefore have a formula which looks like this:

The sales = the food cost + the labour + the overheads.

So, before we look at an example, let's just remind ourselves of our profit calculations.

Profit   = Sales less Costs

Gross Profit   = Sales less Cost of food/drink (goods sold)

$$\text{Gross Profit \%} = \frac{\text{Gross Profit}}{\text{Sales}} \times 100$$

Net Profit   = Sales less Total Costs

Or

Net Profit   = Sales less (food costs/drink costs + labour costs + overheads)

$$\text{Net Profit \%} = \frac{\text{Net Profit}}{\text{Sales}} \times 100$$

Example

An engagement party for 65 guests has selected a buffet, with a food cost of £4.80 per head. In addition, they have requested a disco at a cost of £180, and table decorations and balloons at a cost of £40. Champagne for the toast and wines with the meal will be charged as per consumption, and an additional labour charge of £120 to cover banqueting staff brought in for the function (over and above the kitchen staff preparing the meal) will also be charged.

So we know that sales = food cost + labour + overheads + net profit (where net profit, in this establishment, is expected to be 15% of banqueting sales). What we therefore have is the following formula:

Sales = (4.80 × 65) + £120 + £180 + £40 + net profit (15% of sales)

Sales = £312 + £120 + £180 + £40 + 15% of sales

£120 is made up of 6 banqueting staff for 4 hours @ £5 per hour.

Sales = 652 + 15% of sales (net profit)

Sales (100%) = 652 + 15%

By using a mathematical equation which allows us to give the same treatment to both sides of the equation, we are able to calculate the following, by deducting the 15% from the left-hand side, as well as the right-hand side, of the equation:

If sales (100%) = 652 + 15%
Sales less 15% = 652
85% = 652
So, if 652 = 85%

$$\text{Then } 100\% = \frac{652}{85} \times 100 = £767$$

The Selling Price is therefore £767 + VAT

£767 × 17.5% + = £901
or
£767 × 1.175 = £901

£901 divided by 65 will give us the price per head, which the hotel must charge for the party, which is £13.86p per head.

It is possible to use a straightforward food costing formula to arrive at a selling price for a banquet or a function, but you have to be aware that each individual banquet or function will have its own particular demand, for example flowers, bands, discos, toast masters and so on, so you may be able to calculate the food cost, apply a Gross Profit % of say, 60%/65%, then add on any 'extras', such as the band and flowers, and calculate the selling price that way.

Exercise 1

An hotel has allocated the following proportion of hotel fixed costs to the Function Suite:

Rent & Rates	24 750
Wages/Salaries	61 500
Repairs & Renewals	5 400
Depreciation	12 600
Miscellaneous	5 250
	109 500

The banqueting manager has agreed a menu with a client who is holding a function for 100 people, and has estimated the direct costs of the proposed function as follows:

Food Costs	495
Additional Staff	165
Further Variable Costs	
(electricity, gas, linen, laundry)	90
	750

Question

How much is this function going to cost the client per head, assuming that the banqueting manager is expected to make a net profit on each function of 15%? In other words, what price should the hotel charge per cover?

Answer

The annual Fixed Costs of the function suite amount to £109 500. As the function suite is open and available 365 days per year, then the daily overhead cost is £109 500 ÷ 365 = £300.

The Variable Costs of the proposed function amount to £750, so the Total Cost of providing this function will be £300 + £750 = £1050, or £10.50p per head.

To achieve a Net Profit of 15%, we must, therefore, set a selling price of:

$$\frac{£1050}{85} \times 100 = £1235.29p \text{ which} = £12.35p \text{ per head}$$

To this price, we must add VAT at the current rate.

£12.35 × 1.175 = £14.51 (let's call it £14.55) per head.
Or
£12.35 × 17.5% + = £ 14.51

What if?

What if the banqueting client comes back and says that the maximum he can pay, net of (excluding) VAT, is £9.75 per head? What if, because of the timescale, it is too late for the banqueting manager to 'sell' the suite to anyone else?

Question   If the banqueting manager lost the sale, what effect would that have on the profit or loss of the function suite?

Answer   If the banqueting manager decided not to accept the lower price, and therefore no function is held that day, then the function suite will show a loss for the day of £300 (being the function suite fixed costs of £109 500 divided by 365).

Question   What reasons would there be for accepting or rejecting the client's proposed maximum price?

Answer   However, if the banqueting manager accepts the lower price per head of £9.75 (excluding VAT) then the variable costs will remain at £750, but the sales revenue will amount to £975 (9.75 × 100). This would, therefore, be a contribution of £225 towards the Fixed Costs of the Function Suite, and so the loss for the day will be £75, as against £300 if no function is held. It would therefore be prudent, and better for the overall profitability of the function operation, if the banqueting manager were to accept the booking at the lower price!

STUDENT EXERCISE

1 The annual fixed costs of the banqueting department of the Station Hotel are as follows:

Rates	£16 000
Wages and Salaries	£80 000
Repairs and Maintenance	£11 000
Depreciation	£15 000
	£122 000

A net profit of 17% is required from the banqueting department.
A local charity wants to run a fundraising buffet supper and they have chosen a menu with a food cost of £6.80p for 250 covers.
Extra costs for this function will be £325.

■ Fix a selling price to cover all costs and profit required, inclusive of VAT.

■ What is the lowest price (including VAT) that you could charge?

2 What must the 'contribution' cover when using the contribution method of pricing?

11
Controlling Your Prices

With proper business planning, in any hospitality business, you will have calculated appropriate profit margins and set selling prices accordingly.

Today there is immense competition for customers in every sector of the hospitality business, and clever and sometimes aggressive marketing tactics are required to maintain customers and to encourage new customers.

However, beware of the folly of dropping the price(s) and under-cutting your competitors to attract business, unless you are fully aware of all your current facts, figures and budgets that contribute to your performance to date, and unless you are satisfied that all fixed overheads are paid.

Where is the sense or logic in reducing the selling price when this, in turn, reduces the Gross Profit margin? Remember, all expenses have to be deducted before you arrive at a net profit before tax (or if you're not careful, a net loss before tax). This is an act of desperation. It is also an act of gross stupidity, which for the small independent operator can cost them their business.

Where a larger organisation or chain is concerned, it is a method they may be accused of using as subsidies from other units can absorb the initial short-term loss.

By contrast, increasing your prices will naturally increase your Gross Profit which, after having deducted your expenses, should increase your Net Profit before tax. But what will your customers think of a price increase? How can you justify a price increase to your customers? For whatever reason or justification you have for increasing your prices, how many of your customers are price sensitive and will therefore take their custom elsewhere?

Remember that there is no difference between 10 meals at £20 per head, as against 20 meals at £10 per head, **if the same gross profit formula is applied**.

Your market

If a Gross Profit of 65% is required and the selling prices above include VAT, let's analyse the two examples.

1 10 meals at £20
2 20 meals at £10

Selling price of £20 meal excluding VAT is £20 ÷ 1.175
$$= £17.02p$$
Selling price of £10 meal excluding VAT is £10 ÷ 1.175
$$= £8.51p$$

If gross profit percentage required is 65%, then food cost percentage must be 35% (as both must add up to 100%).

£17.02	= 100%	= Selling Price
£8.51	= 100%	= Selling Price

So

17.02 × 65%	= 11.06	= Gross Profit
8.51 × 65%	= 5.53	= Gross Profit

Therefore

$$17.02 \times 35\% \quad = 5.96 \text{ Food Cost}$$
$$8.51 \times 35\% \quad = 2.98 \text{ Food Cost}$$

$$17.02 \times 100\% = 17.02 = \text{Selling Price}$$
$$8.51 \times 100\% \quad = 8.51 \quad = \text{Selling Price}$$

So, by selling 10/20 meals, the scene is as follows:

Selling Price $10 \times 17.02 = £170.20$
$20 \times 8.51 \ = £170.20$

Food Cost $10 \times 5.96 \ = £59.60$
$20 \times 2.98 \ = £59.60$

Gross Profit $10 \times 11.06 = £110.60$
$20 \times 5.53 \ = £110.60$

Expenses are £100 per day

Therefore, net profit is £10.60

The main issue here is the market in which you operate. If you have been attracting a clientele who pay £20 for food which you purchase at £5.96 per head, then it is unlikely that they would be able to compare this favourably with paying £10 for food which you purchase at £2.98p. In fact, each scenario belongs to a different market.

You could, of course, sell the £20 meal at £10 and keep the food cost of £5.96p, but you wouldn't last long in business.

Remember too that out of Gross Profit we must pay many overheads, including labour.

There is, therefore, a greater proportion of Gross Profit allocated to labour costs for the £20 meal due to more highly skilled/trained staff than for the £10 meal.

Starting a price war

A new establishment opens up round the corner and is offering a menu at £18.50p inclusive of VAT.

We are going to respond by offering our existing £20 menu at the reduced price of £17.50p. Let's see what this does to our profitability.

Selling price of the meal, excluding VAT is

$$£17.50p \times \frac{7}{47} = £14.89p$$

If Gross Profit required is 65%, then food cost percentage must be 35% (as both must add up to 100%)

£14.89p = 100% = Selling Price

But we are offering our £20 menu with just the selling price reduced.

Selling Price = £14.89p

Food Cost (unchanged at £5.96p) = £5.96p

Gross Profit = £14.89p − £5.96p = £8.93p

The question here is how much has the reduction in selling price affected our Gross Profit %?

Let's remind ourselves of the formula.

$$FC\% = \frac{FC}{SP} \times 100, \quad \frac{5.96}{14.89} \times 100 = 40\%$$

$$GP\% = \frac{GP}{SP} \times 100, \quad \frac{8.93}{14.89} \times 100 = 60\%$$

So, instead of achieving the required GP% of 65% by reducing the selling price to £17.50p, we have only achieved a GP% of 60%, down 5%.

So, by selling 50 meals per day, the scene is as follows:

Selling Price 50 × 14.89 = 744.50
Food Cost   50 × 5.96 = 298.00
Gross Profit 50 × 8.93 = 446.50

Let's compare this with our original selling price of £20 per meal.

Selling Price, excluding VAT, is £17.02p

Food Cost is £5.96p and Gross Profit is £11.06p, where FC% = 35% and GP% = 65%

Selling Price 50 × £17.02p = £851

Food Cost   50 × £5.96 = £298

Gross Profit 50 × £11.06 = £553

You can see that selling 50 meals at £17.02p produces a GP of £553, whereas selling 50 meals at £14.89p produces a GP of £446.50p.

In fact, you have to sell 62 meals at £14.89p (producing a GP of 62 × 8.93 = £553.66) to achieve the same gross profit as 50 meals at £17.02p (producing a GP of 50 × 11.06 = £553). This represents an increase of 24% on customer numbers. It is a risk that some operators may consider taking, but to increase customer numbers by 24% from day one is ambitious. Be warned!

If you try reducing your price and do not succeed in attracting the extra business, then your GP%, and subsequently your NP%, will be reduced.

So, to recap:

If you reduce your selling price from £17.02 to £14.89, but keep the same menu and thus food cost, the following happens.

Example 1	Example 2
Selling Price = £17.02 Food Cost = £ 5.96 Gross Profit = £11.06	Selling Price = £14.89 Food Cost = £ 5.96 Gross Profit = £ 8.93

Gross Profit expressed as a percentage of the Selling Price is therefore as follows:

$$\frac{11.06}{17.02} \times 100 = 64.9 \text{ (say 65\%)}$$

$$\frac{8.93}{14.89} \times 100 = 59.9 \text{ (say 60\%)}$$

The selling price has been reduced by 12.5%, i.e.,

$$\frac{(17.02 - 14.89)}{17.02} \times 100$$

$$\frac{2.13}{17.02} \times 100 = 12.5\%$$

So a 12.5% price reduction has resulted in a reduction of 5% in gross profit (60% and not 65%).

In reality, a less expensive restaurant is likely to be a more popular type of restaurant, where the Gross Profit percentage might be at the lower end of the scale, perhaps 60%. Because it is a more popular (affordable) price, then more people will use it more often than, say, a much more expensive restaurant, which may only be used by expense account customers or for 'special occasions'.

The more expensive restaurant will set a Gross Profit percentage higher than the popular one – for instance 68%, because the staff will perhaps be more highly trained, they will have a wine waiter for wines only and they will have silver cutlery, crystal glasses and porcelain plates. In other words, the overheads are more expensive.

Let's say that the table d'hôte menu in the more expensive restaurant is £30 per head.

Middle Market Food Operation		Up-Market Food Operation	
	%		%
Sales 30 000 × £10 = £300 000	= 100%	Sales 10 000 × £30 = £300 000	= 100%
Food Cost 30 000 × 4.0 = 120 000	= 40%	Food Cost 10 000 × 9.60 = £96 000	= 32%
Gross Profit = 180 000	= 60%	Gross Profit = 204 000	= 68%
Expenses = 135 000		Expenses = 159 000	
Net Profit = 45 000		Net Profit = 45 000	

What can we tell from the above figures?

You can deduce that depending upon which market you are in or aiming to attract, you will have to price and plan profit margins accordingly.

What is interesting to note here is that each food operation achieved a net profit of 15% on sales, calculated as follows:

$$\frac{45\ 000}{300\ 000} \times 100 = 15\%$$

Yet, the middle market restaurant had to sell 30 000 meals to achieve this, whereas the up-market operation only had to sell 10 000 meals.

So marketing, as well as pricing and profit margins, has to be right in order to achieve positive results.

STUDENT EXERCISE

1 If your total sales are £8400 (excluding VAT) per week from selling 500 meals at a GP% of 71%, how many more meals must you sell per week to make the same GP margin if you reduce your price by 10%?

2 In another way to increase sales, a consultant has suggested that you offer a free 125cl glass of wine costing 60p to every customer. This results in 100 extra customers in a week, taking the total number of customers to 600. Has this promotion been successful?

12
Identifying Lost Profit

Where does it go?

There are a few struggling businesses left in the hospitality sector who live under the misconception that you can run your business for a year, send your accounts to your accountant, and get them back 6 months later, that is 18 months from the day you started that particular accounting period. Those days are gone now and we can no longer afford to wait for financial information. How can you possibly rectify a financial problem in your business if it takes you 18 months to identify it?

We analyse the Profit and Loss account in greater detail in Chapter 14. Below you will see a list of how profits can evaporate and we will take each one in detail and explain what might happen in any particular business. You can lose profit in the following ways:

1 You do not sell enough (attract enough profit).
  Every time you sell a meal for £10 you are attracting a certain percentage of that £10 which is Gross Profit. From that Gross Profit you have to pay for overheads, some of which are the same however many meals you sell, which will ultimately be deducted from your Gross Profit to leave you your Net Profit. It stands to reason, therefore, that you will lose profit if you do not attract enough sales containing that Gross Profit.

2 You will lose profit if your overheads, such as your rent, rates, motor expenses, labour, electricity, gas and so on, increase dramatically. They then have to be deducted from the Gross Profit which, in turn, is deducted from the sales. So if either your Gross Profit goes down or your expenses go up, you may create a loss or a reduced Net Profit at the end of the period.

If your Gross Profit percentage is reduced, then what you think you are attracting in terms of Gross Profit percentage as a percentage of your sales will not be the case. Remember the example in Chapter 11 when we reduced the price of our meal from £20 to £17.50p, and this reduced our GP% from 65% to 60%, which in 'cash in the bank' terms is as follows. Selling 300 meals per week (50 meals per day × 6 days) × 52 weeks.

Selling Price £20 excluding VAT £17.02p		Selling Price £17.50p excluding VAT £14.89p	
Annual Sales 15 600 × 17.02	= £265 512	Annual Sales 15 600 × 14.89	= £232 284
Less Food Cost 15 600 × 5.96 (Representing 35%)	= £ 92 976	Less Food Cost 15 600 × 5.96 (Representing 40%)	= £ 92 976
Gross Profit	£172 536	Gross Profit	£139 308

The Gross Profit is reduced by £33 228 over the year!

If your Gross Profit percentage is less than it should be, this could be for the following reasons.
- The purchase price of your raw materials has increased and you have not passed that increase on to the customer.
- The recipe you are using to make any or all of the dishes is not being followed and therefore more ingredients than necessary are being used.
- The yield per dish is less than it should be, that is instead of getting 10 portions from a gateau, you only get 9.
- Food is being pilfered at any point throughout your control system.
- Food is being consumed by the customer, but your control system is lacking to the extent that the customer is not being charged correctly.

Have you ever been out for a meal or a snack and ordered something and found that when you ask for the bill either the puddings or perhaps a bottle of wine or a round of beers, is missing?

We won't go into any moral dilemmas on the subject, but somebody, or something, somewhere in the establishment has gone wrong and thus profit is affected.

These are the main reasons for the loss of profit. It is therefore vitally important that you keep a tight rein on the control of every aspect of your business.

You should therefore be reconciling your sales with your purchases, what you are holding in stock and therefore your Gross Profit on a monthly basis. If you do this and the figures don't add up, then if you have a problem which you have highlighted after a month, you can do something about it now rather than wait 6 months, a year or even 18 months!

Ways to lose Gross Profit

Purchase price

In Chapter 7 we calculated that if we were to sell our table d'hôte meal inclusive of VAT at £16.95p, and if our required Gross Profit was to be 62%, our food cost must not exceed £5.48p.

What if we did not monitor what we were buying or we gave out portions that were a little too large, and we didn't notice that over a period of two weeks the average food cost of our two-course table d'hôte meal had increased by 36p (was £5.84 instead of £5.48)? What difference would this make to our Gross Profit and our Gross Profit percentage, which we have calculated at 62%? Let's investigate.

In our original calculations in Chapter 7 we had calculated that the selling price, exclusive of VAT, was £14.43p.

We also calculated that the Food Cost was £5.48p and the Gross Profit was (SP) less (FC), that is £14.43p − £5.48p = £8.95p.

$$FC + GP = SP$$
$$£5.48p + £8.95p = £14.43p$$

In this new scenario, FC + GP must still equal Selling Price.

So, if the new food cost has increased by 36p, the GP must have decreased by 36p because you are still charging the same selling price of £14.43p.

So,
$$FC + GP = SP$$
$$£5.84p + ? = £14.43p$$

£14.43p minus £5.84p = new GP of £8.59p
£8.59p being 36p down on £8.95p

So, the question now to be answered is what is the new GP%? This is calculated as follows:
Remember the formula.
If Selling Price has been set (£14.43p), then the formula is:

$$GP\% = \frac{GP}{SP} \times 100$$

$$= \frac{8.59}{14.43} \times 100 = 59.53\%$$
$$\text{(call it 60\%)}$$

To prove this,

$$FC\% = \frac{FC}{SP} \times 100$$

$$= \frac{5.84}{14.43} \times 100 = 40.47\%$$
$$\text{(call it 40\%)}$$

$$FC\% + GP\% = 100\%$$
$$40.47 + 59.53 = 100$$

So, a lack of monitoring or tight control has reduced our GP% from 62% down to 60%.

Let's say we average 700 covers a week.

Sales: $700 \times 14.43 = 10\ 101$
Less Food Cost 38%   3 838

GP (62%)   **6 263**

Sales: $700 \times 14.43 = 10\ 101$
Less Food Cost 40%   4 040

GP (60%)   **6 061**

The Gross Profit is therefore reduced from £6263 per week to £6061 per week, a difference of £202 per week. If you calculate that over a year, it will reduce your GP% by 2% over the year, or $202 \times 52 = £10\ 504$. That means you have £10 504 *less* to pay your wages and all other expenses. So don't expect a pay-rise this year, because the figures are in fact £10 504 down and all because food cost has gone up by 36p per head in this case!

Standard recipe use

If you do not use standard recipes with accurate ingredients, then the cost of producing the dish will be far greater than the costings on which the selling price was calculated. In addition, if the recipe produced is a dish that is fundamentally different from the one before or the one after, then there is no consistency and no 'standard'. That's when you will hear the customer saying 'It's not as good as it was last time' or 'There's more/less meat than there was last time', and so on.

Portion control

Remember in Chapter 7 we had an apple pie which cost us £5.36p to make. This apple pie gave us 8 portions which we sold at £1.91 per portion, representing total sales of $8 \times £1.91p = £15.28p$, giving a GP of
$£15.28p - £5.36p = £9.92p$ or 65%.

So, someone does not portion the pie correctly and we only get 7 portions.

Total sales now: $7 \times £1.91p = £13.37p$.

GP of $£13.37p - £5.36p = £8.01p$ or 60%

$£1.91p$ lost which equals 5% Gross Profit.

Remember too, that scoops, ladles, trays or weighing scales are all implements we can use for portion control. If a kitchen manual says use a specific spoon or ladle for serving a portion of vegetables or soup for example, then use them. You use measures in the bar for drinks, so why not use measures for the preparation of food!

Pilfering

If goods are bought, but not sold, they will not attract profit. At whichever point throughout the cycle from purchase to sale that goods are pilfered, there will be a loss of profit.

If a portion of apple pie is pilfered after it has been cooked, there will be just the same loss as there would be if the cooking apples were pilfered before the baking took place. This applies to every single item that is purchased for your business.

Free food

If a member of the waiting staff omits to write an order down onto a check-pad, or omits to enter an order into the computer terminal, somebody will not be charged for something they have consumed.

But, as it is something that has been purchased, and therefore has to be paid for, the profit is lost.

Waiters' check pads/computerised point of sale (PoS) system

Many establishments now use PoS systems where the control of stock, and therefore the control of profit, is computerised.

A small PoS system might consist of just one or two cash registers, plus software, a kitchen printer and a computer (PC).

In this way, as the information is entered into the till in the restaurant or at the bar, as well as logging this on to the customer's bill, whatever is entered is automatically deducted from stock.

This replaces the more tedious and labour intensive world of writing down orders for food and drinks on a duplicate or triplicate check-pad, all copies of which are 'married-up' and eventually checked in the 'control office'. As fast as technology moves, new, improved and cost-effective systems come onto the market, which will almost certainly replace the need for illegible scrawls to go orbiting round an hotel. More on computerised systems in Chapter 16.

STUDENT EXERCISE

A packed lunch comprises the items shown below:

	Cost
2 rounds of ham sandwiches	see below
1 apple	16p
1 chocolate biscuit	15p
1 packet of crisps	23p
1 boxed drink	30p
wrapping, bag and napkin	6p

The sandwich ingredients and costs are as follows:

Bread	2 slices per round	Loaf 60p – 20 slices
Butter	15 grammes per round	250gm block 87p
Ham	57 grammes per round	Ham £4.85 per kilo

1 What is the total cost of the packed lunch?
2 What must the customer be charged if the required Gross Profit percentage is 50%?
3 If the sandwich filling is changed to smoked salmon, what is the new profit percentage if the selling price remains the same?
Filling per round: 57 grammes smoked salmon @ £11.00 per kg.

13
Final Accounts, The Trading, Profit and Loss Account and the Balance Sheet

Introduction

At the end of every day in your establishment you could work out what your sales were. You would take that from the till, from your book, or however you record your sales, and you could work out all the costs that were involved, such as how much you paid yourself, how much you paid the bank in interest if you borrowed money in order to establish a business, how much it cost you to buy in the beers, the food, how much VAT you owe, and much else. However, to do this 365 times a year seems a little excessive and what ought to happen is that you should be calculating this every month. By doing so, this will help you to manage your business and by the end of 12 months, which is the acceptable trading account for any business, it should come as no surprise what your profit, or sadly your loss, might be for the year. At the end of the year it is normal practice for your business records to be sent to your accountant, where they are finally calculated and you are presented with two different statements, your profit and loss account for the year and your balance sheet for the day which is the final day of your trading year.

You should be very, very interested in your final accounts because your bank manager, the rest of your colleagues, any potential investors, any partners that you have in business or the tax inspector, will be very interested in your accounts. Don't be someone who thinks that accounts look the same upside down as they do the correct way up. Spend some time reading this chapter and you will realise that the interpretation of accounts is not such a complex process. You need to be able to read and understand them because you need to know how profitable your business was, or is, or how successful it's going to be in the future.

Understanding your accounts will help you to plan ahead, it will allow you to rectify any weaknesses you have and more importantly, it will allow you to exploit the strengths you actually have. Your bank manager will be very interested, as will any other lenders, because they will wish to see your accounts to see whether or not they are going to grant you loan facilities, overdraft facilities, grants, and so on. Any partners or investors will want to know whether or not your suggestion of joining them is a viable proposition, and they are not putting their money into a great empty void. The Inspector of Taxes will be looking to assess your income and on the basis of that, assess your tax liability. There is no way out.

Here is a quick run through an interpretation of accounts.

First, a bit about **Debtors** and **Creditors**. People seem to get confused about what is a Debtor and what is a Creditor. A Debtor, according to Collins' *Concise English Dictionary*, is 'a person or commercial enterprise that owes a financial obligation'.

From time to time debts may be identified as having little prospect of being paid, in which case they become bad debts. This is the exception, rather than the rule, but can become a problem if you do not chase your debts.

If you have provided goods and services and sent out a bill (invoice) which remains unpaid after the agreed time lapse (30 days/60 days) then you must ask for the money – you must control the credit which you are giving to customers.

A Debtor is someone to whom you extend credit.

So, a Creditor is someone who has extended credit to you.

Let's look at this via the illustration of Mr Clarke, the butcher, who supplies your hotel with meat and who also eats regularly in your hotel restaurant.

You ask him as a supplier to supply you on credit. In other words, you ask him to send in an invoice at the end of each month and so gain one month's credit (you don't pay for the goods for 1 month or because the food was ordered at the beginning of the month, you don't pay for it for at least 30 days). This means that Mr Clarke becomes one of your Creditors, because you owe him money. So, in this context, he is your Creditor, but you are his Debtor.

Conversely, when Mr Clarke comes in to eat in your restaurant (which he does every Friday night) he asks if you will send him an invoice at the end of each month. In other words, he asks you if you will supply him with one month's credit. This means that Mr Clarke becomes one of your Debtors, because he owes you money. So in this context, he is your Debtor, but you are his Creditor.

The next often perplexing financial hurdle to overcome after Debtors and Creditors is that of assets and liabilities, but this can be well illustrated by using the Debtor/Creditor scenario.

Let's remind ourselves that a Creditor is someone **to whom** you owe money. This, therefore, means that you have a duty or **liability to pay** them.

On the other hand, a Debtor is someone **who owes** you money, therefore, you have money due to you which is indeed an **asset**.

If you study any balance sheet, you will always find Debtors and Creditors amongst other assets and liabilities.

Final accounts are as follows.

The Trading and Profit and Loss Account

Whether you trade horses, pieces of copper piping or fish and chips, the first calculation you are interested in is the trading account – the calculation made from the prime reason for your trading, the calculation of profit from the buying and selling of the horse, copper pipe or fish and chips.

Once you have calculated the Gross Profit from the trading account, you need to establish whether the expenses you incurred during your trading activities produced a profit or a loss at the end of the period. This is done by deducting all trading expenses (labour and overheads) from the Gross Profit, and is known as the Profit and Loss Account.

These are very often shown together as the Trading and Profit and Loss Account.

The balance sheet

A balance sheet will accurately reflect what a business owns and what a business owes at a particular point in time (the day it was prepared, always, by implication, the last day of the trading account period).

If you fully understand the ratios and percentages which you can extract from your accounts year on year, you will have far greater control over your business, and you will be able to apply appropriate treatment as required to keep your business profitable.

If in a business assets (what it owns) are less than its liabilities (what it owes) then technically it is insolvent and ought to be closed down.

The Profit and Loss (P&L) and the balance sheet

At the end of any accounting period you choose, you can produce a Profit and Loss account and a balance sheet.

You could, and should, in larger businesses, produce 'a profit and loss account, bank balance and debtors position' at the end of each month, and where a book-keeping system is computerised, such monthly accounts are relatively easy to produce.

This will help you to manage your business, and most importantly will allow you to highlight strengths and weaknesses so that appropriate action can be taken immediately (perhaps within a month) and not at the end of 12 months. (In some cases after 12 months it's too late to take corrective action as the problems have been compounded to such an extent that the business fails.)

Figures need to be as accurate and as up to date as possible for them to have maximum impact on your future business performance.

How often you produce figures is a matter of need and discipline, but the taxman (the law if the company has limited liability status) states that at the end of each 12 month period (trading year) a set of accounts must be produced in order that various tax liabilities can be assessed. This generally involves the presentation of a Trading and Profit and Loss account and a balance sheet.

So, before we look at examples of both a trading and a P&L account and a balance sheet, let's explain just exactly what they are and what they represent.

A Trading and Profit and Loss Account is a summary of everything that has been sold or traded (sales) less the cost of the goods which you bought for resale (cost of goods sold) and the operating expenses of trading.

The difference between the two (sales less cost of goods sold) will reveal the Gross Profit, from which you have to deduct your expenses for the period (in this case a year). Remember when calculating the cost of goods sold that the cost of any stock you have at the beginning of the period will have to be added to your purchases for that same period, and that any stock you have at the end of the period will have to be deducted.

There is sometimes some confusion about this, but if you take a step back and think about it, it is really quite simple.

The stock you have at the beginning of the period is likely to have been sold before the end of the period (especially if the period is, say, a year). If you don't account for this, it will look as though you have bought less than you actually have, which means you will have an inflated Gross Profit figure.

Conversely, if you do not deduct what you have in stock at the end of the period (because if it's in stock you haven't sold it yet, therefore it cannot attract profit) your Gross Profit will appear less than it actually is and you might be crying unnecessarily!

By deducting the expenses from the Gross Profit, you will be left with the Net Profit (if the expenses are less than the Gross Profit), or net loss (if the expenses are greater than the Gross Profit).

Figure 13.1 shows the Trading and Profit and Loss account for the Village Tea Shop for year ending 31 December 1996. The Village Tea Shop is run by husband and wife team Kenneth and Helen Thompson.

THE VILLAGE TEA SHOP

Trading and Profit and Loss Account for Year ending 31 December 1996

Sales		**60 000**
Less cost of goods sold		
Stock at 1/1/96	6 000	
Purchases	30 000	
	36 000	
Stock at 31/12/96	9 000	
		27 000
Gross Profit		**33 000**
Expenses		
Gas	960	
Electricity	1 440	
Rates	6 300	
Motor Expenses	4 500	
Advertising	600	
Telephone	1 620	
Insurance	3 600	
Bad Debts	2 100	
Depreciation	6 000	
		27 120
Net Profit		**5 880**

Figure 13.1 *A Trading and Profit and Loss Account*

Interesting though that information is, we can learn much more about the performance and trends of the business if we compare this year's figures with last year's. Thus, in Figure 13.2 we have this year's figures (1996) on the right-hand side of the page, and down the left-hand side we have last year's figures (1995). This is common accountancy practice, apart from Year 1 of any business which has nothing to compare with (although you should, in that case, be comparing budget figures with those actually achieved). More on budgets in Chapter 16.

THE VILLAGE TEA SHOP

Trading and Profit and Loss Account for the Year Ended 31 December 1996

1995			1996
48 000	**Sales**		**60 000**
	Less Cost of Goods Sold		
4 800	Stock 1/1/96	6000	
27 600	Purchasing	30 000	
32 400		36 000	
6 000	Stock 31/12/96	9 000	**27 000**
26 400			
21 600	**Gross Profit**		33 000
	Expenses		
500	Gas	960	
750	Electricity	1 440	
5 220	Rates	6 300	
3 600	Motor Expenses	4 500	
	Advertising	600	
1 160	Telephone	1 620	
2 000	Insurance	3 600	
60	Bad Debts	2 100	
3 000	Depreciation	6 000	
16 290			27 120
5 310	**Net Profit**		**5 880**
2 655		2 940	
2 655		2 940	
5 310		5 880	

Figure 13.2 *Accounts for two consecutive years*

The £5310 net profit in 1995 was split equally between Kenneth and

Helen, £2655 each, and the £5880 net profit in 1996 was also split equally, £2940 each.

Let us also look at the balance sheet for the Village Tea Shop as at 31 December, where you will see this year's balance sheet (1996) on the right-hand side of the page, compared with the 1995 balance sheet on the left-hand side. Figure 13.3 shows the Thompson's balance sheet.

THE VILLAGE TEA SHOP

Balance sheet as at 31 December 1996

	Fixed Assets	Cost	Depreciation	Written Down Value (WDV)
1995				
240 000	Land & Buildings	240 000	–	240 000
15 000	Fixtures & Fittings	30 000	6 000	24 000
15 000	Motor Vehicles	30 000	3 000	27 000
270 000		300 000	9 000	291 000
	Current Assets			
6 000	Stock	9 000		
3 600	Debtors	3 000		
38 820	Cash	300		
48 420		12 300		
	Current Liabilities			
300	Creditors	600		
600	Accruals	300		
	Bank Overdraft	6 000		
900		6 900		

		Partner A	Partner B	
47 520	**Net current Assets**			5 400
317 520	**Net Assets Employed**			296 400
	Financed by	**Partner A**	**Partner B**	
330 210	Capital 1/1/96	158 760	158 760	317 520
5 310	Profit	2 940	2 940	5 880
335 520		161 700	161 700	323 400
18 000	Drawings	13 500	13 500	27 000
317 520	Capital 31/12/96	148 200	148 200	296 400

Figure 13.3 *A balance sheet*

Analysing accounts

Let us now take our time and analyse some of the percentages and ratios which we can extract from the Trading and Profit and Loss Accounts and from the balance sheets for the two years. You will be amazed at the amount of vital information you can extract.

Gross Profit

In 1995 the Gross Profit was £21 600 on sales of £48 000
In 1996 the Gross Profit was £33 000 on sales of £60 000
So our Gross Profit is up from £21 600 to £33 000, an increase of £11 400.
So let's find out what Gross Profit percentage we achieved in each year and compare them.

For 1995 we want to express £21 600 as a percentage of £48 000. The formula is as follows:

$$\frac{21\ 600}{48\ 000} \times \frac{100}{1} = 45\%$$

Let's compare that with our 1996 Gross Profit percentage, where we want to express £33 000 as a percentage of £60 000.

The formula is as follows:

$$\frac{33\ 000}{60\ 000} \times \frac{100}{1} = 55\%$$

So our Gross Profit has increased by 10% and what we can now do is investigate further and find out the reason why.

Sales

Let's look first at the sales and compare 1995 with 1996.

Sales have increased from £48 000 to £60 000, an increase of £12 000.

Expressed as a percentage increase on 1995, this is an increase of 25%

$$\frac{12\ 000}{48\ 000} \times 100 = 25\%$$

So, if our sales have increased, it stands to reason that our cost of goods sold or purchases have increased.

We can see that this has increased from £26 400 to £27 000, an increase of only £600, which, expressed in percentage terms, is 2.27% (let's say 2%).

As sales have increased by 25%, we would expect the cost of these goods sold to increase by more than 2%.

There are many reasons, however, to explain this relative decrease in the cost of goods sold.

■ Buying in bulk and therefore negotiating cheaper prices. This could also explain the relatively high closing stock which we will look at shortly.

■ Smaller portions are being given.

■ Wastage or theft may have reduced, thus making the operation more profitable.

Stock turnover

Here is an interesting ratio.

If we take the average stock at any one time and multiply by 52 (weeks in the year) and then divide by the cost of goods sold, we will discover the length of time stock is held. This will also tell us the number of times stock is replenished in any given period (in this case, over a year).

The calculations for this for 1995 are as follows:

Average stock calculation

Stock at 1/1/95 = 4 800
Stock at 31/12/95 = 6 000

Average stock therefore is (4 800 + 6 000) ÷ 2 =
10 800 ÷ 2 = 5 400

The stock turnover is thus calculated as

$$\frac{5\ 400 \times 52}{26\ 400\ (\text{cost of goods sold})} = 10.63\ (\text{let's say } 10.5)$$

This means that in 1995 stock was replaced every 10 and a half weeks.

In 1996, however, the calculation is as follows:

Average stock calculation

$$\text{Stock at } 1/1/96 = 6\,000$$
$$\text{Stock at } 31/12/96 = 9\,000$$

Average stock therefore is $(6\,000 + 9\,000) \div 2 =$
$$15\,000 \div 2 \qquad = 7\,500$$

The stock turnover for 1996 is therefore

$$\frac{7\,500 \times 52}{27\,000 \text{ (cost of goods sold)}} = 14.44 \text{ (let's say } 14.5)$$

This means that in 1996 stock was replaced every 14 and a half weeks.

This increase from 10 and a half to 14 and a half weeks means that stock is now being held for over 3 months on average!

Even with bulk buying, this is a long time to keep goods, especially if deliveries can be made weekly or fortnightly.

For a food operation, especially where a lot of fresh produce is used, you would expect a high turnover of stock at least every one or two weeks. So, reducing stock levels becomes a major priority for this business.

Let's now turn our microscope onto the net profit of the business.

Net Profit

The Net Profit is what a business is left with after the cost of sales and all other expenses (excluding tax) have been deducted from the sales.

In 1995 the Net Profit was £5310 against sales of £48 000.

In 1996 the Net Profit was £5880 against sales of £60 000.

So the respective Net Profits expressed as a percentage of sales are as follows:

1995 $\dfrac{£5310}{£48\ 000} \times 100 = 11.06$ (let's say 11%)

1996 $\dfrac{£5880}{£60\ 000} \times 100 = 9.8$ (let's say 10%)

Our Net Profit is down 1% and this is despite an increase in our Gross Profit of 10% as shown in the following account.

	1995		1996	
Sales	100%	48 000	100%	60 000
Less cost of goods sold	55%	26 400	45%	27 000
Gross Profit	45%	21 600	55%	33 000

Remember Gross Profit + cost of goods sold must always add up to 100% (sales).

If we then express the expenses and the Net Profit as a percentage of sales we will see why our Net Profit has reduced. Next, let's take a look at the Net Profit % calculations.

	1995		1996	
Sales		48 000		60 000
Less cost of goods sold		26 400		27 000
Less expenses	45%	16 290	34%	27 120
Net Profit	10%	5 310	11%	5 880

So we can see that there has been an increase in expenses from £16 290 to £27 120, an increase of 11%.

At this stage in an analysis of a Profit and Loss Account, the expenses should be thoroughly investigated. Let's examine the expenses in more detail.

Power (Gas and Electricity)

From £1250 in 1995 to £2400 in 1996 is an increase of 92%.

This could be due to additional equipment (see balance sheet) or longer opening hours (producing increased sales) or wastage.

Think about how often you have seen the kitchens heated first thing in the morning by turning on all the gas hobs and/or ovens!

Rates

Here we see an increase of 20.68% (say 21%).

Beyond your control perhaps, but you should at least have known in advance.

Motor expenses

These have increased from £3600 to £4500, an increase of £900 or 25%.

This is probably due to the additional motor vehicle (see balance sheet) purchased during the year which would require additional running expenses (insurance, road tax and so on).

Advertising

The fact that no advertising was done in 1995 and £600 has been spent in 1996 would explain the increase in sales.

Telephone

An increase of £460 (over 39%) suggests that further investigation is required.

This is a very high telephone bill for a restaurant. Perhaps it is being used for purposes other than business by the owners and staff!

Insurance

An increase of £1600 representing 80% is probably due to the purchase of additional equipment during the year (see balance sheet).

Once again, this figure is very high and requires further investigation.

Bad debts

The increase of £2040 or 3 400% is extraordinarily high. This figure should be checked to see whether the debts really are bad debts and that such an amount is unlikely to be recovered.

Depreciation

Depreciation has increased from £3000 to £6000, an increase of 100%.

Easily explained from the balance sheet as the fixed assets have increased from £30 000 to £60 000, an increase of 100% (the fixed assets being fixtures and fittings and motor vehicles).

You will note that as part of the **Fixed Assets** Land and Buildings is not depreciated. This is because historically land and buildings have increased in value (appreciated) from year to year, although more recently this has not always been the case.

Depreciation

Let's explain depreciation and make it simple. When goods are bought to be used in a business, but are not bought for the prime purpose of reselling (for instance motor vehicles, refrigerators, computers) they are known as **Fixed Assets**.

As fixed assets wear out with use do not last forever, and sooner or later will have to be replaced, the value of these fixed assets decreases. There comes a point at which these assets are replaced with new 'models', the original ones either being sold 'second hand' or scrapped.

The profit and loss account is charged each year with a portion of the cost of fixed assets, such as equipment, fittings and motor vehicles, to reflect the use of these assets in earning profits for a business.

So what do we do with this 'loss' of value? Let's take the example of a house purchase to illustrate the point.

This charge is called depreciation and has the effect of reducing the cost of an asset to zero or scrap value over the years of its working life in the business.

Because depreciation only applies to certain fixed assets, any losses incurred can be charged to the Profit and Loss Account and depreciation is an expense which can therefore be charged in the same way that we charge electricity, wages and so on – as a cost to our business.

So, if you buy a van for the business for £15 000 and sell it 10 years later for £1500, then over 10 years the van has cost you £13 500 or £1350 per year.

This means that depreciation of £1350 will be charged each year to the Profit and Loss Account and the value of the asset will be reduced each year by £1350 in the balance sheet.

So, the van is a **cost** to the business and a **depreciating asset**.

In general, depreciation can be calculated by two different methods:
- ■ the Straight Line Method;
- ■ the Reducing Balance Method.

Straight Line Method

Estimate the useful life time of the asset (number of years of use) and estimate the value of the asset at the end of its useful life time.

The formula is as follows:

$$\frac{\text{Cost} - \text{Disposal Value}}{\text{Number of Useful Years}}$$

Let's say a van is purchased for £14 400 and it is estimated that it will be disposed of in 4 years' time for £900.

Using the Straight Line Method, let's depreciate it over 4 years.

$$\frac{£14\,400 - £900}{4} = \frac{£13\,500}{4}$$

$= £3375$ each year for 4 years

Reducing Balance Method

This way a fixed percentage for depreciation is deducted from the cost in year one. In year 2, and subsequent years, the same percentage is deducted from the previously reduced balance.

Let's use the van, bought for £14 400 and charge depreciation at 50% per annum. After 4 years the calculation would be as follows:

	Cost		£14 400
Year 1	Depreciation 50%		£ 7 200
		Balance	£ 7 200
Year 2	Depreciation 50%		£ 3 600
		Balance	£ 3 600
Year 3	Depreciation 50%		£ 1 800
		Balance	£ 1 800
Year 4	Depreciation 50%		£ 900
		Balance	£ 900

By comparing these two methods of depreciation, we can see that the Reducing Balance Method has a higher charge for depreciation in years 1 and 2, but lower charges in years 3 and 4. However, it is probable that motor repairs will be much higher in years 3 and 4 than in years 1 and 2, which may well 'straighten out' the figures charged to the Profit and Loss Account.

So, let's now take a look at our balance sheet and, using more ratios, let's analyse our business performance.

Fixed Assets

Kenneth and Helen Thompson have a lot of money invested in Fixed Assets.

In 1995, the fixed assets generated £48 000 turnover (18%)

This is calculated by taking the turnover (sales) and dividing it by the total of the fixed assets.

$$\frac{48\ 000}{270\ 000} \times 100 = 17.7\% \text{ (call it 18\%)}$$

In 1996 the turnover has increased to £60 000, but with increased fixed assets (£291 000) which means the ratio is up to 21%.

Is this trend from 18% to 21% good or bad?

It's getting better, because a return on fixed assets of 21% $\left(\frac{60\ 000}{291\ 000}\right)$ is marginally better than 18% $\left(\frac{48\ 000}{270\ 000}\right)$ but arguably, business efficiency is based upon achieving the maximum turnover from assets which, at present, are only returning a relatively low turnover. It would appear that the assets are being under-utilised and seem to be lying idle most of the time (that is, they are only yielding 18p for every £1 invested).

The Thompsons should sell any unused assets and before buying any new equipment careful consideration should be given to what the asset will be used for.

Return of Capital Employed (ROCE)

The return of capital employed provides us with a good overall view of the strength of any business. It measures the business's profit against the resources under its control.

The present rate of ROCE is:

1995: $\frac{5310}{317\ 520} \times 100 = 1.67233$ (call it 1.7)   1996: $\frac{5880}{296\ 400} \times 100 = 1.98380$ (call it 2.00%)

So, in this case, the ROCE has increased from 1.7% in 1995 to 2.0% in 1996.

Although we should be glad to see this increase, the return is unacceptable.

If the worth of the net assets employed had been invested in a high deposit bank account or building society, then the interest generated at, say, 4%, would have been £296 400 × 4% = £11 856, which is a significant improvement on the present business performance.

The ROCE should be greater than this to compensate for the stresses and worries of being in business for yourself.

Liquidity

When we test for our current viability, we should look at our current assets and see how quickly and easily we can convert them into ready cash.

This should be compared with our current liabilities to give us our liquidity ratio:

$$\text{liquidity} = \frac{\text{Current Assets}}{\text{Current Liabilities}}$$

The 1995/96 Balance Sheet shows our current assets (stock + debtors + cash) as follows:

	1995	1996
Stock	6 000	9 000
Debtors	3 600	3 000
Cash	38 820	300
	48 420	12 300

and our current liabilities (Creditors, Accruals and Bank Overdraft) as follows:

	1995	1996
Creditors	300	600
Accruals	600	300
Bank Overdraft	000	6000
	900	6900

So in **1995** $= \dfrac{48\ 420}{900} = 53.8 : 1$ **1996** $= \dfrac{12\ 300}{6900} = 1.78 : 1$

There is a significant drop from 1995 to 1996, due to the purchase of fixed assets and also due to the purchase of large quantities of stock.

In 1996, however, the ratio indicates that the Thompsons have £1.78 in current assets to match every £1 of current liabilities.

However, as most liabilities are paid for from cash which is in the bank or from money coming in from debtors paying their accounts, and as our other calculations have shown that the stock is taking 14.5 weeks to turn into cash, let us ignore stock for this next calculation and look at . . .

The Acid Test Ratio

$$\text{Acid Test Ratio} = \dfrac{\text{Current Assets less Stock}}{\text{Current Liabilities}}$$

The Acid Test Ratio shows the ability of the business to meet its current commitments and will be affected by the following factors:

The ratio will be reduced if:
1 the business makes losses or becomes less profitable;
2 fixed assets are purchased;
3 loans or capital are repaid.

The ratio will be increased if
1 profits are increased;
2 fixed assets are sold;

3 new capital is issued;

4 new **long term** loans are negotiated.

So, by ignoring stock in the calculation, the ratios are again from the balance sheet as follows:

1995	1996
$$\frac{\text{Current Assets less Stock}}{\text{Current Liabilities}}$$	$$\frac{\text{Current Assets less Stock}}{\text{Current Liabilities}}$$
$$\frac{48\,420 - 6000}{900}$$	$$\frac{12\,300 - 9000}{6900}$$
$$= \frac{42\,420}{900} = 47:1$$	$$\frac{3300}{6900} = 0.48:1$$
$$1995 = \frac{42\,420}{900} = 47:1$$	$$1996 = \frac{3300}{6900} = 0.48:1$$

So, in 1995 we could certainly meet our liabilities using this Acid Test Ratio (£47 in liquid cash for every £1 of liabilities), but in 1996 we only have 48p in liquid cash to pay for every £1 of liabilities we have.

This business, therefore, is clearly lacking in working capital.

Credit Given (Debtors Turnover)

$$\text{Formula} = \frac{\text{Annual Debt}}{\text{Annual Sales}} \times 365 = \text{X number of days credit given}$$
$$1995 \; \frac{3600}{48\,000} \times 365 = 27 \text{ days} \qquad 1996 \; \frac{3000}{60\,000} \times 360 = 18 \text{ days}$$

This ratio reflects Debtor control, allowing customers to pay later for goods and services can severely disrupt your cash flow.

By keeping a tight control on credit, cash can be unlocked into the business and so reduce finance charges and thus improve profits.

The trend of this ratio can prove quite revealing, and in the above example, the trend is good. We can see that Debtors are settling their accounts on average, within 18 days, which is an improvement on the 27 days in 1995. To improve the cash flow position even more, credit transactions should be discouraged.

Credit Taken (Creditors Turnover)

$$\text{Formula} = \frac{\text{Credit}}{\text{Purchases}} \times 365 = \text{X days given}$$

$$\textbf{1995} \quad \frac{300}{27\,600} \times 365 = 4 \text{ days} \quad \textbf{1996} \quad \frac{600}{30\,000} \times 36 = 7 \text{ days}$$

This business is now taking 7 days instead of 4 days to pay its suppliers.

Ideally, we would like our Debtors (18 days 1996) to pay us faster than we pay our Creditors (7 days 1996). In general, the more credit that can be taken, the better – provided it is within our agreed trading terms. However, we should strive to take advantage of discounts offered for prompt payment.

A good reputation for prompt payment is almost always beneficial to a business. Adopting a more casual approach to owing money can be less helpful, as it is Creditors who are usually instrumental in bringing down an ailing business.

So, what does all this ratio analysis tell us about this business? What do we conclude from comparing all these figures?
- We conclude that this business is slowly deteriorating with reducing profit margins and little working capital.
- The property has far greater potential and capacity than is currently being utilised.
- In order to survive, the Thompsons must dig deep into their management skills and address their marketing, selling, production, prices, competitors and customer demand.
- But at least they are utilising financial controls which are keeping them abreast of their current situation and the trends emerging from their trading patterns.

■ Perhaps the owners should consider moving to smaller premises, which are better suited to operating on a smaller scale, thus requiring a lower capital investment.

STUDENT EXERCISE

You have been approached by Rob Collins, who is looking for you to invest £20 000 in his restaurant in return for a directorship.

Examine the figures from the documents shown below and on pages 141–146. Does Rob's Restaurant offer a sound investment?

ROB'S RESTAURANT LIMITED

BALANCE SHEET
AS AT 31 MARCH 1997

	Notes	1997 £	1997 £	1996 £	1996 £
FIXED ASSETS					
Tangible Assets	5		83 974		81 100
CURRENT ASSETS					
Stock		6 280		7 696	
Debtors		9 778		5 918	
Cash at Bank and in Hand	6	280		1 656	
		16 338		15 270	
CREDITORS					
Amounts due within one year	7	60 118		69 178	
NET CURRENT LIABILITIES			(43 780)		(53 908)
TOTAL ASSETS LESS CURRENT LIABILITIES			40 194		27 192
CREDITORS					
Amounts due in more than one year		38 640		35 214	
			38 640		35 214
			1 544		(8 022)
CAPITAL & RESERVES					
Called Up Share Capital			100		100
Profit and Loss Account	8		1 354		(8 022)
			1 454		(8 122)

.... }

R. COLLINS   }

                                             } **DIRECTORS**

                                             }

.... }

A. FERGUSSON

Approved by the Board on 29 July 1997

ROB'S RESTAURANT LIMITED

NOTES TO ACCOUNTS
FOR THE YEAR ENDED 31 MARCH 1997

1. **ACCOUNTING POLICIES**

   a) The Accounts have been prepared under the Historical Cost convention.

   b) Turnover represents the net amount of invoices to customers less credit notes for goods returned, excluding VAT.

   c) No depreciation is provided on Freehold Land and Buildings which, in the opinion of the directors, have a value in excess of their cost.
   Depreciation is provided on other assets in equal instalments over their useful lives. The following rates have been applied:

Vehicles	20%
Fixtures and Fittings	10%

   d) Stock and Work in Progress is valued at the lower of Cost and Net Realisable Value after making due allowance for obsolete and slow-moving items.

   e) Deferred Taxation is provided at the current rate of Corporation Tax on the excess of Book Written Down Value of Plant and Vehicles over their Tax Written Down Value.

2. **TURNOVER**

   The turnover and loss before taxation is attributable to the Company's principal activity, namely that of a restaurant.

3. **OPERATING (LOSS)/PROFIT**

   The Operating (Loss)/Profit is stated after charging:

	1997 £	1996 £
Amounts written off Tangible Assets	2 862	2 874
Directors' Remuneration	33 266	23 430
Auditors' Remuneration	800	800
Staff Costs (Note 4)	32 668	30 630
Bank Interest	1 454	6 258
Credit Card Charges	2 852	2 942

4. **STAFF COSTS**

	1997	1996
	£	£
Salaries and Wages	29 180	27 906
National Insurance Costs	3 488	2 724
	32 668	30 630

The average weekly number of employees during the year was as follows:

	No.	No.
Directors	3	3
Sales	3	5

5. **FIXED ASSETS**
Tangible Assets

	Motor Vehicles	Plant & Equipment	Property	Total
COST	£	£	£	£
At 1 April 1996	1 000	26 738	59 118	86 856
Additions in Year	–	–	–	–
Disposals in Year	–	–	–	–
At 31 March 1997	1 000	26 738	59 118	86 856
DEPRECIATION				
At 1 April 1996	208	2 674	–	2 882
Write Off On Disposal	–	–	–	–
Charge for Year	200	2 674	–	2 874
As at 31 March 1997	408	5 348	–	5 756
NET BOOK VALUE				
At 31 March 1997	592	21 390	59 118	81 100
At 31 March 1996	792	24 064	59 118	83 974

6. **DEBTORS**

	1997	1996
	£	£
Amounts due within one year		
Trade Debtors	9 778	3 344
Prepayments	–	2 574
	9 778	5 918

7. **CREDITORS**

	£	£
Amounts due within one year		
Bank Account	4 310	13 632
Loans	1 600	4 120
Trade Creditors	29 384	25 340
PAYE	4 810	3 472
Accruals	3 150	4 502
Directors' Loan Account	8 330	10 870
Value Added Tax	8 534	7 242
	60 118	69 178
Amounts due after more than one year		
Bank Loan Account	38 640	35 214

Bank loan and overdraft is secured by a charge over the company's assets.

8. **CALLED UP SHARE CAPITAL**

	1997	1996
	£	£
Authorised : Ordinary Shares of £1 each	100	100
Allotted, issued and fully paid ordinary shares of £1 each	100	100

ROB'S RESTAURANT LIMITED

TRADING & PROFIT & LOSS ACCOUNT
FOR THE YEAR ENDED 31 MARCH 1997

	1997	1996
	£	£
Sales	219 788	206 830
Cost of Sales	97 552	86 278
Gross Profit	122 236	120 552
	55%	58%
Less Expenses		
Salaries & Wages	32 668	30 630
Motor & Travel	3 744	786
Equipment Leasing	698	648
Repairs/Renewals	1 644	1 566
Cleaning/Laundry	3 844	4 792
Telephone	1 632	1 350
Entertaining	1 108	2 534
Printing & Stationery	1 994	1 240
Advertising	6 552	11 476
Crockery & Cutlery Renewal	1 088	1 248
Heat & Light	5 382	5 610
Kitchen Accessories	1 344	1 662
Disposables	2 504	3 020
Insurances	1 922	1 732
Rent & Rates	2 346	3 382
Accounting	1 000	1 000
Consulting Fees	–	11 426
Book-keeping	2 810	1 840
Credit Card Charges	2 852	2 942
Bank Charges	1 098	920
Sundry Expenses	1 682	2 214
Directors' Remuneration	32 006	20 668
Directors' Pension Scheme	1 260	600
Auditors' Remuneration	800	800
Bank Interest	1 454	6 258
Depreciation	2 622	2 874
Loss on Sale of Asset	240	–
	116 294	130 128
Net (Loss)/Profit for Year	£5 942	£(9 576)

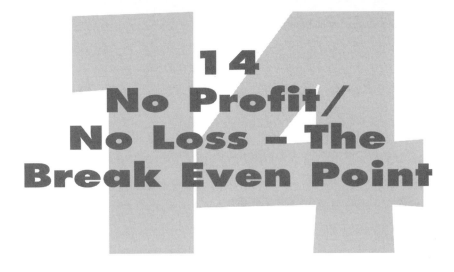

14
No Profit/
No Loss – The
Break Even Point

A popular misconception

Many people have aspirations to own their own hospitality business – be it a pub, hotel, restaurant, café or bunk house – selling accommodation, food and drink in a variety of guises. Some of the above establishments will sell only one of those items listed above, whilst another will sell two or three of the above hospitality components.

Once you have a business idea, you have to turn it into a profitable business. You have to calculate a few figures and away you go.

Let's take a look at Oliver Rattlecliff's business idea. He wants to start a ready-made meal supply business called Wheel and Freezers and has come up with the following costings for his first two dishes of Chicken Tikka Masala and Chilli Con Carne.

He has worked out that it will cost him approximately £1000 to produce 60 mixed cases (1200 portions) of Chicken Tikka Masala and Chilli which he can sell for £33.30p per case. This means that Oliver's weekly sales, costs and profit forecasts were as follows:

Sales	60 × £33.30p	£2000
Costs		£1000
Profit		**£1000**

So, at the prospect of making £1000 per week, Oliver starts the business.

The production of the dishes went well and he sold the goods at £33.30p per case. The only minor problem was that he was only able to sell 30 cases a week and not the 60 he had originally planned.

Oliver, therefore, revised his figures accordingly, by a process of mere simple division

Sales	30 × £33.30	£1000
Costs		£ 500
Profit		£ 500

In other words, if the profit on £2000 of sales was £1000, then the profit on £1000 of sales must be £500.

A popular misconception! Where have Oliver's calculations gone wrong? He has made a fundamental mistake in the correlation between costs and profit.

Fixed and variable costs

We referred to fixed and variable costs earlier in the book in Chapter 9. Let us examine them in a bit more detail:

Sales £2000

PROFIT £1000		Sales £1000	
		Profit	£200
Distribution	£100	Distribution	£50
Containers/Packaging	£100	Containers/Packaging	£50
Food Cost	£200	Food Cost	£100
Wages	£400	Wages	£400
Overheads	£100	Overheads	£100
Factory Unit	£100	Factory Unit	£100

Figure 14.1 *Fixed and variable costs*

Initially it looks as though there are 6 different kinds of costs – *Factory Unit, Overheads, Wages, Food Cost, Containers* and *Distribution.* In fact, there are only two kinds – variable costs and fixed costs.

Variable costs

Oliver has to pay for the raw food, containers, packaging and part-time labour only when he is actually cooking batches of food. The amount he pays out varies directly with the number of portions (or cases) produced. Twenty less portions (one less case) and he uses less raw food, less containers and packaging and he sends the part-time packer, Mrs Boite, home early.

If, on the other hand, Oliver was to produce an extra case or two, he will use more food and packaging and he will ask if Mrs Boite can come in for an extra few hours.

Those are, therefore **variable** costs, which he only has to pay when he is cooking and packaging the meals.

Fixed costs

The Factory Unit (rent and rates), the office lighting, heating, telephone (the overheads) have to be paid, whether Oliver produces 1 case, 10 cases or none at all.

In addition, skilled chefs are in great demand, so he will have to keep them permanently on the payroll, or he'll lose them to another employer. They have, in fact, become a fixed cost, and fixed costs have to be paid regardless of the level of business.

The lesson

Once you break down Oliver's costs in Figure 14.1 into fixed and variable, you can see where he was caught up in a popular misconception. When he halved his meal production from 60 to 30 cases, and therefore his sales from £2000 to £1000, it was only his variable costs (distribution, containers and packaging and food) that were halved from £400 to £200. His fixed costs stayed exactly as they were at £600.

So, when production was halved, and sales dropped from £2000 to £1000, his profits weren't halved. They were reduced from £1000 to £200, a drop of 80%!

So, the lesson here for Oliver is as follows:

If he looks back on his first year's business because he is using these figures to help produce his budgets for the following year, he will see that he has produced 2000 cases of Wheel and Freezer products at a total cost of £33 300.

It would be a mistake for Oliver to assume that the production costs of one case are therefore £16.65p. The costs **were** £16.65p in the previous period, and they were £16.65p because Oliver produced 2000 cases. With 4000 or 7000, the cost per case would be different. So, to go into next year, assuming his costs, per case, will still be £16.65p, is incorrect.

A look at contribution and marginal costing

Oliver should have carried out a proper form of costing, which we call **marginal costing**. It is best illustrated by looking at Oliver's mum's business.

She runs her home as a Bed and Breakfast in Bournemouth, where Oliver's dad and his younger brother and sister also live.

Mrs Rattlecliffe reckons it costs £140 per week for Council Tax, food, electricity, gas, insurance and telephone

£140 ÷ 4 members of the family, or, £35 per head.

So, what Mrs Rattlecliffe wants to know is, what the extra cost would be if a Bed and Breakfast customer comes to stay. It is not another £35, because the Council Tax and the Insurance do not go up. Electricity, gas and telephone go up a little and food goes up quite a lot.

So Mrs Rattlecliffe concludes that if a Bed and Breakfast customer came for a week, the cost of running the house would go up from £140 to £161. So the marginal costing is £21 per week or £3 per night.

The first thing any business must do is separate the variable costs from the fixed costs.

Let's go back to Oliver at Wheel and Freezers and look at his weekly fixed costs.

Wages	£400
Overheads (including rent & rates)	£200
	£600

His variable costs, per case, were as follows:

Food Cost	£3.30
Containers/Packaging	£1.70
Distribution	£1.30
	£6.30

This makes £6.30 the variable cost per case.

If you deduct this from the selling price of £33.30p per case, then you are left with the figure of £27.00 for each case.

So, the £27 per case is not profit, especially if we have fixed costs of £600 per week still to be paid. The £27 is a contribution to the £600 fixed costs. When all the fixed costs are paid, this £27 will become a contribution to profit.

The above contribution concept feeds directly into the theory of marginal costing. By using this approach, it enables business planners to see what effect selling one, 500, or 1000 more cases, meals and rooms will have on their profits.

So, in Oliver's business, his fixed costs are £600 and his contribution per case is £27. If he can produce and sell 23 cases per week, he will have a profit of £21 (27 × 23 = £621). If he produces any more than

23 cases, every single £27 will be pure profit. So, if he can sell 60 cases with a marginal costing of £27, then his profit will be:

60 × 27 =	1600
Less Fixed Costs	600
Profit	1020

This can be proved by the following method:

60 × £33.30p = £1998 sales
Less variable costs of £6.30p per case
60 × £6.30p £ 378
= £1620
Less Fixed Costs £ 600
£1020

Let's explain this graph in Figure 14.2 in simple terms.

Along the bottom axis you have the number of cases – we have gone up to 100 in this example.

Up the left hand side (axis) we have the money scale starting at £100 and going up to £2300.

The dotted line for costs starts at £600, because that £600 is your fixed costs and continues to rise at £6.30p per case. The sales line starts at zero, rises at £33.30p per case and goes up to £2300 and can, in fact, go off the scale if your sales are that good. The break even point is the point where the cost line and the sales line meet. In other words, where costs equal sales – no profit, no loss. Anything after that is pure profit, measured between the cost line and the sales line.

Anything below the break even point is a loss, because you haven't reached the point at which you have paid your fixed costs.

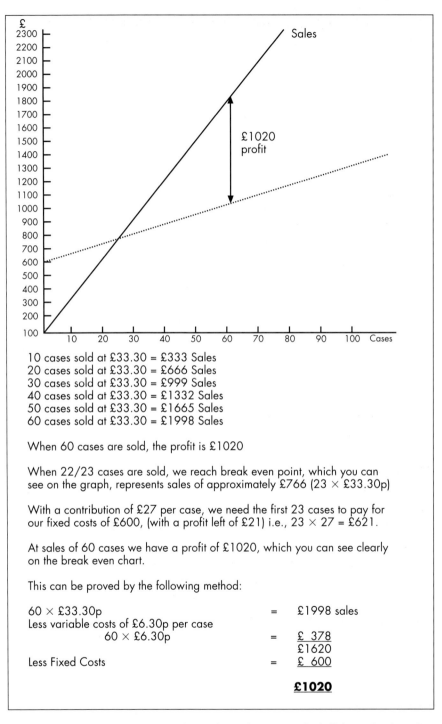

10 cases sold at £33.30 = £333 Sales
20 cases sold at £33.30 = £666 Sales
30 cases sold at £33.30 = £999 Sales
40 cases sold at £33.30 = £1332 Sales
50 cases sold at £33.30 = £1665 Sales
60 cases sold at £33.30 = £1998 Sales

When 60 cases are sold, the profit is £1020

When 22/23 cases are sold, we reach break even point, which you can see on the graph, represents sales of approximately £766 (23 × £33.30p)

With a contribution of £27 per case, we need the first 23 cases to pay for our fixed costs of £600, (with a profit left of £21) i.e., 23 × 27 = £621.

At sales of 60 cases we have a profit of £1020, which you can see clearly on the break even chart.

This can be proved by the following method:

60 × £33.30p	=	£1998 sales
Less variable costs of £6.30p per case		
60 × £6.30p	=	£ 378
		£1620
Less Fixed Costs	=	£ 600
		£1020

Figure 14.2 *Break even analysis for Oliver Rattlecliffe's Wheel and Freezers*

STUDENT EXERCISE

1 Hungry Hugo's is a popular 150 cover restaurant.

Each month it therefore has a capacity of (30 days × 150 covers) 4500 covers.

The average spend is £9.00. The GP% is 64% and the fixed costs are £4600 per month.

How many covers, representing how much in sales, does Hungry Hugo's require to break even? Draw up a break-even chart to illustrate your answer.

2 The Alexander Hotel has accommodation for 180 guests. It has fixed costs of £70 000 per month.

The average spend, per guest, is £55 per night, with a variable cost of £7.50p per guest, per night.

Draw up a break even chart to show the number of guests required monthly for the Alexander to break even.

If the Alexander has 3900 guests over one month, how much profit does it make?

15
Basic
Budgets

According to Collins *Concise English Dictionary*, the word 'budget' is derived from a fifteenth century French word meaning a leather pouch or wallet! It has more than one meaning:

1 an itemised summary of expected income and expenditure over a specified period;

2 the total amount of money allocated for a specific purpose during a specified period.

To prepare a budget, you work out all the sources of income (rooms, food, bars, and so on), all the costs and areas of expenditure and decide what you think you will sell and for what price(s) you think you will sell.

You need a sheet of paper and a pencil, a PC if you're a larger organisation, consultation with your colleagues or heads of department/managers and a bit of good judgement.

There are very few businesses nowadays who can manage their businesses without using budgeting as an important management tool. By preparing a budget, you are setting the standards of the performance you expect to achieve for the period ahead.

In essence, a business will forecast income and expenditure at least

12 months in advance (in many cases this can be up to 3, 5 and 10 years in advance).

At the end of each month the actual income and expenditure is compared with the budgeted income and expenditure. Any differences in actual against budget will be noted and in this way budgets can be used to control a business – hence budgetary control. This is, once again, another example of the careful planning of a business.

A budget is a means by which a business gets from A to B to help it achieve goals and targets. If we therefore plan to make a specified amount of profit each month, by estimating what our sales, cost of sales, wages, overheads and so on will be, then we can estimate what our balances will be at the end of the year.

By monitoring them monthly with what our actual sales, cost of sales, wages, overheads and so on are, we can control our business by taking action with things that have just happened and take action for future operations.

However, the first thing we have to do is plan our budgets and this involves forecasting, in advance, what our income and expenditure is likely to be over a given time.

If we take as an example the forecasting of, say, sales in a catering establishment, then we will need to base our forecasting on, for example:
- competition – past, present, future;
- expanding or contracting local economy;
- rising, static, falling inflation.

It is worth noting here that if sales are budgeted to grow significantly over a given period, we would expect to see the marketing budget increase to take account of increased advertising activity.

Another example would be in a sales budget for, say, an hotel which recently had another 50 bedrooms built on. Of course, the sales in the sales budget would increase, but so also would the housekeeping wages in the wages budget!

Budgets can be set by individuals and for the smaller operation, need not take days to prepare. However, the larger organisations and the multi-national companies may often bring together key Managers or Heads of Department and form a Budget Committee.

It stands to reason in this day and age of empowerment and devolvement of central decision-making that people who have had input into a budget (that is have been consulted regarding forecasts of revenue and expenditure) are much more likely to use and control the budget successfully than those who have had an operating budget thrust upon them.

There is no end to the number of budgets that an organisation can use to help control and manage its business, but here are the most common forms used in the hotel and catering industry:

■ The Sales Budget;
■ The Departmental Operating Budget;
■ The Operating Budget;
■ The Cash Budget;
■ The Master Budget.

Let's look at the budgets in a bit more detail.

The Sales Budget

Many businesses would consider the Sales Budget to be the most important budget as obviously all other budgets are based upon this.

A business without sales does not exist as a going concern, and the more sales you have, the more profit you will attract (providing, of course, you are selling your goods and services profitably).

In order to complete an accurate Sales Budget, you will require to gather as much market intelligence as possible:

■ all previous year's departmental sales figures;
■ any plans or scope for expansion the business may have;
■ the present and future economic climate, nationally and locally;
■ present, past and future competition for your product or service;
■ any proposed price increases or decreases;
■ what does the Sales Manager/sales team think he/they can do?

The sales that you forecast in your Sales Budget become the revenue targets for that period, but they must be **realistic**. There is nothing more de-motivating for any member of a team, be it a senior or junior member, than trying to achieve unrealistic sales targets.

So, don't look at last year's figures and conclude that because last year's figures were up 4%, you'll go for 5% next year – that's 'wing and prayer' budgeting.

An example of a Sales Budget is shown on page 159.

It goes without saying that each department within an hotel will have its own budget, but the budget of that department will also reflect the mix between different products and their relative prices in that department (for example beers, wines and spirits in a bar).

Example of Sales Budget

The following rates have been agreed for the Parkgate Hotel, a new 80-bedroom hotel, with 6 identical meeting/function rooms, a bar and a Mediterranean style restaurant.

Corporate Accommodation Rate:	£63
Meeting Rooms	£200 per day
Food Average Spend	£11.50p
Weekend Accommodation Rate	£48

The following forecasts have been made for the Parkgate for the first 6 months of the year, January–June, inclusive.

	January	February	March	April	May	June
Corporate Bed Nights	600	650	700	800	700	850
Weekend Bed Nights	70	80	180	250	200	320
Meeting Rooms	30	30	65	75	45	80
Food (covers)	800	900	1045	1225	1000	1350

The sales budget should look like this:

	January	February	March	April	May	June	Total
Corporate Accomm.	37 800	40 950	44 100	50 400	44 100	53 550	270 900
Weekend Accomm.	3 360	3 840	8 640	12 000	9 600	15 360	52 800
Meetings	6 000	6 000	13 000	15 000	9 000	16 000	65 000
Food	9 200	10 350	12 017	14 087	11 500	15 525	72 679
Liquor	6 400	7 200	8 360	9 800	10 560	10 800	· 53 120
Total	62 760	68 340	86 117	101 287	84 760	111 235	514 499

Departmental Operating Budgets

These contribute, as all budgets do, to the master budget, but also fulfil crucially the need of departmental accounting (it's no use knowing at the end of the year that the hotel made a net profit of £25 000 if, in fact, the rooms make a profit of £15 000, the restaurant made a profit of £15 000 and the bars made a loss of £5000). So there you are, congratulating yourself on how profitable your business has been, when you don't know that you have a major problem in the bar.

So by going to the sales budget of the hotel, each department would be able to start making up the Departmental Operating Budget by taking the sales figure off the main sales budget. The costs involved in the operating budget will relate directly to the sales budget and will include cost of sales, direct labour and overheads.

There follows an example of a Departmental Operating Budget.

Example of a Departmental Operating Budget

This would normally be broken down on a monthly basis. Let's look at the Restaurant Operating Budget for the Parkgate Hotel for May.

Budgeted Sales	100%	£15 180
Cost of Sales	38%	£5 768
Gross Profit	62%	£9 412
Labour Cost	21%	£3 188
Direct Expenses (linen, laundry, flowers)	4%	£ 607
Net Operating Profit	37%	£5 617

What if the department has no sales (that is non-revenue earning)?

Where an hotel department is non-revenue earning (for example marketing budget, maintenance budget) then an 'expenditure budget' will be prepared.

In certain cases, expenditure in non-revenue earning departments may be split between the non-revenue earning departments and the capital budget. An example of this would be in the marketing and the maintenance department when, say, a new conference facility was being built onto an hotel. Some of the expenditure for the above would be taken from the marketing and the maintenance budget, whilst the rest would be taken from the capital budget, which can be fully justified as part of the capital cost for the project, as capital expenditure budgets involve budgeting new equipment and services which will increase the worth (asset value) of the business, whilst operating budgets are only concerned with maintaining the existing equipment and services.

The Operating Budget

This is all the sales departmental budgets combined to show the budgeted operating profit for each department and the net profit for the hotel after all direct and indirect overheads and expenses have been deducted.

An example of the Operating Budget of the Parkgate Hotel for the month of May is shown in Figure 15.1 on page 161.

	Rooms		Meeting		Food		Liquor		Total	
	%	£	%	£	%	£	%	£	%	£
Sales	100%	53 700	100%	9 000	100%	11 500	100%	10 560	100%	84 760
Cost of Sales	–	–	–	–	38%	4 370	45%	4 752	11%	9 122
Gross Profit	100%	53 700	100%	9 000	62%	7 130	55%	5 803	89%	75 638
Direct Labour	19%	10 203	20%	1 800	21%	2 415	20%	2 112	19%	16 530
Direct Expenses	20%	10 740	50%	4 500	4%	460	2%	211	19%	15 911
Operating Profit	61%	32 757	30%	2 700	37%	4 255	33%	3 485	51%	43 197

Indirect Expenses:		
Rates & Insurances	5%	4 238
Maintenance	5%	4 238
Marketing	4%	3 390
Administration	5%	4 238
Heat & Light	7%	5 993
Labour	5%	4 238
Depreciation	3%	2 543
	34%	28 878

Budget Net Profit 17%   £14 319

Figure 15.1 *Parkgate Hotel – Operating Budget May 1996*

The Cash Budget

This is exactly what it says – a forecast of the total cash income and expenditure of the business as it flows in and out, based upon all the other operating budgets. It bears many similarities to a business or bank cash flow statement and like a cash flow statement, is usually broken down month by month.

The Cash Budget will show how income from debtors can come into the business one or two months later, but how expenditure such as suppliers may only need to be paid one or two months (30–60 days) after delivery.

On the other hand, wages must be paid immediately at the end of the week or month, and some rent and rates agreements demand payment in advance.

All these transactions and the timing of these transactions will have an effect on your Cash Budget, and throughout the year the availability of cash to spend on capital expenditure will be greatly influenced by what the Cash Budget forecasts are.

Like cash flows, Cash Budgets have a 'nudge-on' effect, so that each month there is an opening balance of cash (the same as the closing balance from the previous month) to which incoming cash is added and outgoing cash is deducted. This will leave a new balance at the end of the month to be brought forward as the opening balance at the beginning of the next month and so on.

An example of a Cash Budget for the Parkgate Hotel Restaurant for the 6 months to end June 1996 is shown in Figure 15.2.

Here are the forecasts:

	Sales	Purchases	Labour	Overheads
January	9 200	3 495	1 930	1 100
February	10 350	3 930	2 175	1 240
March	12 000	4 560	2 525	1 440
April	14 100	5 355	2 960	1 690
May	11 500	4 370	2 415	1 380
June	15 525	5 900	3 260	1 860

In addition:
- 30% of sales are credit sales and are paid the month after;
- all purchases will be paid the month after;
- the balance of cash in the bank on 1 January 1996 is £24 800.

IN	January	February	March	April	May	June
Opening Balance	24 800	26 310	29 405	33 015	37 275	40 405
Cash Sales	6 440	7 245	8 400	9 870	8 050	10 868
Credit Sales	7 000★	2 760	3 105	3 600	4 230	3 450
	38 240	**36 315**	**40 910**	**46 485**	**49 555**	**54 723**
OUT						
Purchases	8 900★	3 495	3 930	4 560	5 355	4 370
Labour	1 930	2 175	2 525	2 960	2 415	3 260
Overheads	1 100	1 240	1 440	1 690	1 380	1 860
Total	**11 930**	**6 910**	**7 895**	**9 210**	**9 150**	**9 490**
Balance C/Fwd	**26 310**	**29 405**	**33 015**	**37 275**	**40 405**	**45 233**

★ These are December figures. The £7000 representing the 30% of sales which were credit sales in December and £8900 being the purchases for December, due to be paid in January.

Figure 15.2 *Cash Budget for Parkgate Restaurant for 6 months to end June 1996*

	Rooms	Meetings	Food	Liquor	Total
Sales	53 700	9 000	11 500	10 560	84 760
Less Cost of Sales	–	–	4 370	4 752	9 122
Gross Profit	**53 700**	**9 000**	**7 130**	**5 808**	**75 638**
Less Expenses &					
Wages	20 768				
Rates & Insurances	7 238				
Maintenance	11 500				
Marketing	4 000				
Administration	6 300				
Heat & Lighting	6 470				
Miscellaneous	2 500				
Depreciation	2 543				**61 319**
				Net Profit	**14 319**

Figure 15.3 *Parkgate Hotel Budgeted Trading and Profit & Loss Account for May 1996*

The Master Budget

The Master Budget is a budgeted Trading and Profit and Loss Account and budgeted Balance Sheet at the end of the accounting period (for budgeting purposes, usually monthly, annually, 3 yearly, 5 yearly, 10 yearly). The Master Budget is an amalgamation of all other budgets and forecasts. Examples are shown in Figures 15.2 and 15.3 respectively.

Once we have made accurate forecasts and have agreed that all our budgets are realistic, we have set our performance standards. What we now have to do is use our budgets effectively to control our business. We will, in fact, measure our actual performance against that for which we budgeted.

The analysis of the comparisons is known as 'variance analysis' – where the variance is the deviation from the standard which could be plus or minus, positive or negative. Increases and decreases in sales will almost always cause an increase or a decrease in costs, but what we must examine is the relativity of such variances.

Fixed Assets		
Land & Buildings	750 000	
Fixtures & Fittings	200 000	
Motor Vehicles	10 000	
	960 000	
Current Assets		
	£	
Stock	26 600	
Debtors	8 400	
Cash	20 000	
	£55 000	
Current Liabilities		
	£	
Creditors	34 000	
Bank Overdraft	18 000	3 000
	£52 000	**£963 000**
Financed by:		
£		
Capital	613 000	
Bank Loan	350 000	**£963 000**

Figure 15.4 *Parkgate Hotel Balance sheet at 1 June 1996*

Such variances will affect our budget and will involve us in taking 3 steps towards controlling our budgets:
- review;
- react;
- revise.

Review

The important point here is to know about budget variances and have sufficient explanation and enough time to do something about them. Time is of the essence!

So, having discovered a variance, you must investigate and find out the cause, whether the variance is up or down. I was working earlier this year with a caterer whose average spend in the restaurant in November went down from £9.40p to £7.80p. The explanations were simple.

■ Heavy snow fell (earlier than usual) one Friday evening and a party of 10 cancelled. This explains the variance in covers – you are unlikely to be 100% accurate in such forecasting, so to get as accurate as this guy got is very good indeed (also lucky).

■ The average spend was really worrying – down from £9.40p to £7.80p, but the explanation was simple.

■ The owner had gone on holiday for two weeks, and during his absence, one of the service staff became ill. A replacement was found who was competent in many aspects of the job, but didn't bother to 'sell' sweets and liqueurs. When the owner returned from holiday, his budgetary control review highlighted the problem and the member of staff was immediately given some coaching and one-to-one training, and believe it or not, the variances for December were positive rather than negative (but it was Christmas).

React

Remember, actions always speak louder than words. If you lose a contract or get a cancellation for a big function or numbers reduce significantly for a dinner dance, then do something! Don't just get angry or feel victimised, *you can't afford to!* This will have implications for your business, so find alternative business and adjust your budgets accordingly.

Revise

■ Remember that using your budgets as a control for your business is all about constant revision.

■ Don't forget that a positive variance needs just as much thought and planning to revise as a negative variance.

■ It is a well-known fact that staff shortages are already occurring in the hotel and catering industry, and a significant increase on budgeted sales could have serious implications if skilled staff cannot be recruited to service this increase!

So let's look at the reasons why variances occur. First of all, **Sales Variances**.

In the food and beverage or accommodation departments, sales variances are caused by the following:

■ more or less customers than budgeted;

■ an increase or decrease in the average spend of these customers;

■ a combination of the two.

Cost Variances are caused by the following:

■ a greater or lesser cost paid for the goods;

■ an increase or decrease in the quality used;

■ a combination of the two.

It stands to reason that an increase in food sales would result in an increase of cost of sales.

The use of flexible budgets will allow us to extract the cost variances which are directly related to a sales variance and those which are not, for example the flexible budget shows cause and effect and therefore only the variances outwith the flexible allowances need further investigation. An example of Sales Variances is shown on page 168, and how those variances are accounted for in a Flexible Budget is shown on page 169.

Sales variances are a direct result of a change in the pattern of customer behaviour. Variances occur when more or less customers, spend more or less money than you forecast for the sales budget. For example, if actual sales are greater than budgeted, it could be a result of more customers spending more money, more customers spending less money, or less customers spending more money. Conversely, if actual sales are less than those in the sales budget, the opposite has happened.

Let's look at this in the example of the Parkgate Hotel Restaurant, and look at the food sales budget for February.

Parkgate Hotel Food Budget, February 1996

	Budget	Actual	Variance
No. of Covers	900	985	+85
Average Spend	£11.50	£12.05	+55p
Sales	£10 350	£11 869	+£1 519

So, this is good news. We have 2 positive variances. Not only are customer numbers up, but average spend is up as well.

By using the flexible budget, we can account for the variances in a slightly different way.

Parkgate Hotel Food Budget, February 1996

	Budget	Flexible Budget	Actual	Variance
No of Covers	900	985	985	+85
Average Spend	£11.50	£11.50	£12.05	+55p
Sales	£10 350	£11 327	£11 869	+£542

i.e., the number of covers variance is:

85 × 11.50 (our original budget figure)= £977

Average spend (over our total number of covers)

$$985 \times 55p \quad = \underline{£\ 542}$$

$$\underline{\underline{£1\ 519}}$$

So, it is two elements of differing customer behaviour, £977 + £542, that have contributed to our total budget variance of +£1519.

An increase in customer numbers and average spend will obviously affect our food cost budgets and, once again, a flexible budget will interpret the reasons for the increase.

Parkgate Hotel Restaurant Food Cost Budget, February 1996				
	Budget	**Flexible Budget**	**Actual**	**Variance**
Sales	£10 350	£11 869	£11 869	
Cost of Sales	£3 933	£4 510	£4 748	+238
Gross Profit (62%)	£6 417	£7 359	£7 121	(−238)

So, the flexible budget tells us that our food cost has risen by £238 over and above the fact that it would have anyway with the increase in covers.

Without the flexible budget, the information would be thus:

	Budget	**Actual**	**Variance**
Sales	£10 350	£11 869	+£1 519
Cost of Sales (38%)	£3 933	£4 748 (40%)	+£815
Gross Profit	£6 417	£7 121	+£704

This tells us that our food cost has gone up, but doesn't tell us whether it is due to the increase in sales and/or the increase in food cost, whereas the flexible budget immediately tells us that, although our sales are up, our Gross Profit is down on budget!

STUDENT EXERCISE

1 You have been asked to prepare a cash budget for the Lampson Lodge Hotel for the second half of 1997, commencing 1 July 1997.

The income and expenditure forecasts are as follows:

Month	Sales	Purchases	Wages	Overheads
May	52 000	21 000	15 000	20 000
June	58 000	20 000	17 000	21 000
July	44 000	13 000	12 000	17 000
August	38 000	12 000	11 000	16 000
September	50 000	18 000	13 000	22 000
October	56 000	17 000	16 000	21 000
November	48 000	18 000	14 000	18 000
December	64 000	19 000	16 000	22 000

NOTES

1 10% of sales are account customers who pay the month after.
2 Suppliers are paid 2 months after the supply month.
3 Labour is paid on the month due.
4 Overheads are paid one month after supply.
5 HMCE (Her Majesty's Customs & Excise) will pay you a VAT refund of £6000 in October.
6 The opening bank balance on 1 July 1997 is an overdraft of £27 000.

2 Accommodation sales for the Mansewood Towers Hotel are forecast to be £7 500 000 for year commencing 1 April 1999. A new environmentally-friendly policy has been adopted by the hotel.
You have been asked to prepare an accommodation operating budget for 1999 from the following information:
1 Labour 15.75% of Sales
2 Direct heat, light and power 7.95% of sales
3 Ozone friendly cleaning materials 2.05% of sales.

3 Total food sales for the first six months of this year (April–September) at Wonderful Winton's Wine Bar were £198 000 from 25 000 customers.
As a result of an aggressive marketing campaign, you are expecting a 4% increase in sales for the first 6 months of next year and you are increasing your prices by 2.5%, neither of which will affect your average customer spend.
Prepare a sales budget for April to September, inclusive, for next year.

16
The Applications of Computers for Costing and Purchasing

Once you have a thorough grasp of the theory and how the 'manual' systems for costing and purchasing work (and you should have, now that you have read this book), you can look at the labour saving ways in which computer programmes can be utilised to speed up many of the processes and take the tedium out of certain repetitive operations.

In addition, many companies will customise software for you (for a price of course).

- Front Office;
- Back Office;
- Food and Beverage Control;
- Point of Sale;
- Conference and Banqueting;
- Leisure and Resorts;
- Human Resources;
- Management Information.

The hospitality industry is now high-tech and offers computer applications covering every operational area within an hotel facility for the large and small operator.

Let us look in a bit more detail how each computer application, or an integrated computerised system, can further tighten controls and thus maximise profitability in the hospitality business.

Front Office computer applications

Reservations

Many systems can handle individual or group reservations with up-to-the-minute information on room type availability, to help up-selling and to help identify any pre-negotiated rates, as well as allowing over-selling to any pre-set ceilings.

Complex billing instructions can also be accommodated to be activated automatically on arrival.

Reception

Software packages can produce arrival reports which ensure that guests have a speedy check-in.

In addition, registration details can be pre-printed which saves time at check-in and reduces queues for group arrivals. Rooms can be allocated automatically or manually. In addition, some applications can split charges between company and guests' own account, and some applications can access the guest history information to ensure speedy check-in for previous guests who have arrived without reservations.

Guest history

Each time a guest checks in or out, software can automatically create a guest record which can enhance customer service and be used for future reservations and promotional mailings.

Cashiering

Both guests and management appreciate accurate billing and many systems nowadays can produce fully supported bills or accounts where credit limits can be checked and payment made by any method, including on-line credit and debit card transactions.

Postcode addressing

The Post Office's postal address file is now utilised by many Front of House computer applications to allow for rapid look up of addresses by postcode. This speeds up guest registration and ensures the consistency and accuracy of guest history for future sales and marketing use.

Telephone/Concierge

There are sophisticated systems on the market which will keep track of guests' messages, and help track guests by capturing point of sale information at dining or leisure facilities.

Such systems can also activate PABX or TV-based message waiting signals and help telephone operators with rapid look up of guests' room numbers.

These systems will also control guest direct dialling and post all call charges to correct guest folios.

Back Office computer applications

Sales and marketing

Many computer databases will analyse buyer and consumer behaviour statistics and reports can be produced showing, for example, occupancy by room rate, locations of businesses, conversion ratios of bookings to registrations and so on, thus highlighting the strengths and weaknesses of your marketing approach. In turn, all this information can help you to attract repeat business, improve occupancy and improve average rates.

Such systems allow mailings to become even more targeted and highly personalised, and such systems can also handle enquiries for other hotel services such as conference and restaurant.

Such systems can also alert operators to call back a potential client at any given time and date and can also monitor the effectiveness or rate agreements.

Yield management

By combining historic analysis with current reservation status, many back office computer programmes have a facility to compare performance against budget for any given period, and also to project likely future business. Such projections can be used to modify rates for any given booking period to optimise profits.

Accounting and financial control

When financial ledgers are fully automated and integrated clerical effort is reduced and cash flow management can be optimised.

Managers have access to an extensive variety of financial reports for measuring and controlling profitability and performance from the sales ledger, purchase ledger and general ledger, including the automatic generation of invoices, statements and aged department reports, automated payments of authorised invoices according to agreed supplier terms and discounts, and profit and loss information from financial ledgers at the touch of a button.

Night audit

Some systems never need to shut down for the night audit, which means posting to folios continues 24 hours a day and performance figures can be available to managers as they report in for duty the next day.

Housekeeping

Usually working in tandem with reception, computerised housekeeping systems keep information on rooms to be serviced at the beginning of the day. As rooms come on stream, some systems allow information to be keyed in from a terminal or via the guest telephone.

If, for any reason, Housekeeping put a room 'out of order' this information is immediately available to Reception, who can immediately alert the Maintenance Department.

Some systems can now even produce a Turn-Down report which indicates the number of guests per room!

Building maintenance

One of the key management objectives in any accommodation business is containing maintenance costs and maximising rooms in service and earning revenue.

Where such a programme is in operation, maintenance managers can allocate jobs and completion dates to withdraw maintenance areas from service, and can use reports to highlight overdue work and any recurring problems.

Food and beverage control

There are now a wide variety of systems available, some of which are able to fully integrate with stock control (inventory control) and Point-of-Sale, in addition to using recipe costing to compare current menu costs with selling prices. Some programmes will also analyse food usage to identify excessive shrinkage.

Purchasing

Accurate up-to-date information on current prices can be instantly available on a computerised system, which helps the purchaser to monitor supplier performance and might even improve a purchaser's bargaining position.

Orders can be generated from, for example, a kitchen terminal, and can reflect exact meal requirements, helping to drive efficiency and reduce wastage.

Receiving

Overall efficiency of any operation can be improved when the stores department know which goods to expect and can take quick action over non-deliveries.

Many computerised control systems are fully integrated, that is, goods received and suppliers' invoices must match before payment is made.

Stores

Again, many integrated packages will track every item of stock held in a single store or multiple outlets and ensure that stores are issued on a first-in-first-out (FIFO) basis.

In addition, re-order quantities are prompted and facilities are available for menu planning, recipe costing and profit forecasting. Some of the menu planning databases will allow you to search for recipes by ingredients, thus allowing you to maximise high stock levels to produce menu 'specials' and so on.

Many software applications now offer 'full recipe item explosion', which, as well as sounding rather colourful can assist the kitchen in the timely presentation of each course and can provide control over multiple location stock levels.

Stock line checks can be carried out and rectified immediately to provide minute by minute stock monitoring information. Closing period stock-take functions can provide comprehensive profit and loss accounts, product by product or group by group.

Glossary

Asset	Anything owned by the business.
Balance Sheet	A summary of what the business owns (value of assets) and what it owes (how it finances the assets). Both must balance, because what a business has, must be paid for!
Break-even Point	The sales level at which you have earned enough revenue to cover all costs. The point in any business where there is no recorded profit, nor no recorded loss.
Capital	Can mean the following: ■ working capital ■ share capital (amount put into a business by the shareholders) ■ the value of fixed assets.
Cash Flow	The pattern of cash coming in and going out of a business, where a surplus or deficit of cash does not indicate that a profit is being made or a loss incurred.
Closing Stock	The value of stock held at the end of any period of business.
Creditor	Somebody to whom you owe money.
Current Assets	Anything owned by a business which can be turned into cash relatively quickly, for example cash, stock, debtors.
Current Liability	The total of a business's short-term debt owed to its creditors, for example unpaid invoices, bank overdrafts.

Debtors   Someone who owes you money.

Depreciation   The cost of a fixed asset spread over its working life.

Fixed Assets   An asset which is in permanent use within a business, for example buildings, furniture.

Fixed Costs   Costs which do not change significantly with fluctuations in sales.

Gross Profit   The difference between the cost and the selling price (excluding VAT) of an item, or between the sales and the cost of those sales during a given accounting period.

Gross Profit Margin   The gross profit expressed as a percentage of the selling price (excluding VAT). Not to be confused with mark-up.

Mark-Up   The gross profit expressed as a percentage of the cost price.

Net Assets Employed   The total value of all assets employed in the business, less short-term liabilities (that is assets financed by owners' capital and/or long-term loans).

Net Profit   The amount left at the end of any given trading period after all fixed costs (overheads and expenses) have been paid for out of Gross Profit.

Opening Stock   The value of stock at the beginning of a trading period.

Trading and Profit & Loss Account   Shows sales and the costs involved in achieving those sales for a given trading period. After deduction of all costs, this account will show a net profit or net loss.

Variable Cost A cost that varies significantly with variations in sales.

Working Capital The amount of money that is used to buy stock to sell for cash, to use to buy the stock again and so on. In accountancy terms, it is found by subtracting current liabilities from current assets.

Formulae/ Useful Information

1 To set the selling price once you know the cost of food or liquor and the required GP%

$$SP = \frac{\text{Food/Liquor Cost}}{\text{FC\%/LC\%}} \times 100$$

2 To calculate the GP% if the selling price has been set and you have calculated the food cost or liquor cost.

$$GP\% = \frac{GP}{SP} \times 100$$

3 To calculate the FC% or LC% if the selling price has been set and you have calculated the food cost or liquor cost.

$$FC\%/LC\% = \frac{FC/LC}{SP} \times 100$$

4 Food Cost + Gross Profit   = Selling Price

5 Liquor Cost + Gross Profit = Selling Price

6 FC%/LC% + GP%   = 100%

7 To add VAT

Net Price $\times$ 17.5% + = Price inclusive of VAT

or

Net Price $\times$ 1.175   = Price inclusive of VAT

8 To deduct VAT from a VAT inclusive price:

Gross Price $\times \dfrac{7}{47}$ = VAT content of Gross Price which should be deducted from Gross Price.

or

Gross Price $\div$ 1.175 = VAT content of Gross Price which should be deducted from Gross Price.

Margin	Markup	Margin	Markup	Margin	Markup
1.00%	1.01%	35.00%	53.85%	69.00%	222.58%
2.00%	2.04%	36.00%	56.25%	70.00%	233.33%
3.00%	3.09%	37.00%	58.73%	71.00%	244.83%
4.00%	4.10%	38.00%	61.29%	72.00%	257.14%
5.00%	5.26%	39.00%	63.93%	73.00%	270.37%
6.00%	5.38%	40.00%	66.67%	74.00%	284.62%
7.00%	7.53%	41.00%	69.49%	75.00%	300.00%
8.00%	8.70%	42.00%	72.41%	76.00%	316.67%
9.00%	9.89%	43.00%	75.44%	77.00%	334.78%
10.00%	11.11%	44.00%	78.57%	78.00%	354.55%
11.00%	12.36%	45.00%	81.82%	79.00%	376.19%
12.00%	13.64%	46.00%	85.19%	80.00%	400.00%
13.00%	14.94%	47.00%	88.68%	81.00%	426.32%
14.00%	16.28%	48.00%	92.31%	82.00%	455.56%
15.00%	17.75%	49.00%	96.08%	83.00%	488.24%
16.00%	19.05%	50.00%	100.00%	84.00%	525.00%
17.00%	20.48%	51.00%	104.08%	85.00%	566.67%
18.00%	21.95%	52.00%	108.33%	86.00%	614.29%
19.00%	23.46%	53.00%	112.77%	87.00%	669.23%
20.00%	25.00%	54.00%	117.39%	88.00%	733.33%
21.00%	26.58%	55.00%	122.22%	89.00%	809.09%
22.00%	28.21%	56.00%	125.27%	90.00%	900.00%
23.00%	29.87%	57.00%	132.56%	91.00%	1011.11%
24.00%	31.48%	58.00%	138.10%	92.00%	1150.00%
25.00%	33.33%	59.00%	143.90%	93.00%	1328.57%
26.00%	35.14%	60.00%	150.00%	94.00%	1566.67%
27.00%	36.99%	61.00%	156.41%	95.00%	1900.00%
28.00%	38.89%	62.00%	163.16%	96.00%	2400.00%
29.00%	40.95%	63.00%	170.27%	97.00%	3233.33%
30.00%	42.86%	64.00%	177.78%	98.00%	4900.00%
31.00%	44.93%	65.00%	185.71%	99.00%	9900.00%
32.00%	47.06%	66.00%	194.12%	100.00%	
33.00%	49.25%	67.00%	203.03%		
34.00%	51.52%	68.00%	212.50%		

Pounds to grammes and kilos conversion factors

1oz	= 28	Grammes
2ozs	= 57	Grammes
3ozs	= 85	Grammes
4ozs	= 113	Grammes
5ozs	= 142	Grammes
6ozs	= 170	Grammes
7ozs	= 198	Grammes
8ozs	= 227	Grammes
9ozs	= 255	Grammes
10ozs	= 284	Grammes
11ozs	= 312	Grammes
12ozs	= 340	Grammes
13ozs	= 369	Grammes
14ozs	= 397	Grammes
15ozs	= 425	Grammes
16ozs	= 454	Grammes

$\frac{1}{2}$lb	= 227	Grammes		
1lb	= 454	Grammes		
2lbs	= 907	Grammes		
3lbs	= 1361	Grammes	= 1.361	Kilogrammes
4lbs	= 1815	Grammes	= 1.815	Kilogrammes
5lbs	= 2268	Grammes	= 2.268	Kilogrammes
6lbs	= 2722	Grammes	= 2.722	Kilogrammes
7lbs	= 3439	Grammes	= 3.439	Kilogrammes
8lbs	= 3629	Grammes	= 3.629	Kilogrammes
9lbs	= 4083	Grammes	= 4.083	Kilogrammes
10lbs	= 4536	Grammes	= 4.536	Kilogrammes

50 Grammes	= 1.76	Ounces
100 Grammes	= 3.53	Ounces
150 Grammes	= 5.29	Ounces
200 Grammes	= 7.05	Ounces
250 Grammes	= 8.81	Ounces
300 Grammes	= 10.58	Ounces
350 Grammes	= 12.34	Ounces
400 Grammes	= 14.11	Ounces

450 Grammes	=	15.87	Ounces	=	1lb
500 Grammes	=	17.63	Ounces		
550 Grammes	=	19.40	Ounces		
600 Grammes	=	21.16	Ounces		
650 Grammes	=	22.92	Ounces		
700 Grammes	=	24.69	Ounces		
750 Grammes	=	26.45	Ounces		
800 Grammes	=	28.22	Ounces		
850 Grammes	=	29.98	Ounces		
900 Grammes	=	31.74	Ounces	=	2lbs
950 Grammes	=	33.51	Ounces		
1000 Grammes	=	35.27	Ounces		

Index